BLACK&DECKER®

Mar. 23, 2011

Here's How

WINDOWS

Big Savings at a Bargain Price

Creative Publishing international

MINNEAPOLIS, MINNESOTA
www.creativepub.com

Contents

INTRODUCTION 5

1 New Window Sash 8

2 Framing & Installing Windows 12

3 Garden Windows 22

4 Bay Windows 26

5 Glass Block Windows . . . 36

6 Skylights 40

7 Tubular Skylights 50

8 Basement Egress Windows 52

9 Patio Doors 58

10 Stool & Apron Window Trim 64

11 Basement Window
Trim 68

12 Replacing Broken
Window Glass 72

13 Improving Window
Operation 76

14 Replacing Insulated
Glass Units 80

15 Fixing Sliding Screen
Doors 84

16 Repairing &
Maintaining Storm
Windows 86

17 Weatherizing 90

18 Detecting Energy
Loss 92

19 Replacing Storm Windows 95

Introduction

Few remodeling jobs have a greater impact on the livability and value of your home than replacing, adding or repairing windows. There are many paybacks: improved home value, better security, lower energy costs, increased light and ventilation, and added curb appeal. Best of all, if you have moderate tool skills, window projects are well within your reach, saving you considerable costs over having the work done by contractors.

Unlike the larger, more expensive volumes, this book doesn't include background information on cutting holes in walls or expanding living areas. What it does do is give you step-by-step information on how to change the look of your home by installing different types of windows.

Want to add some indoor greenery? Check out the Garden Window on page 22. Need to add some privacy to a bathroom while still allowing some natural light? Turn to page 26 to see how to install a glass block window. Looking for a way to add some light to a dark interior room? The skylight project on page 40 may be just what you're looking for.

And if you aren't ready to replace a window just yet, there are steps that can be taken to repair or improve operation of your current windows. There's even a section on inexpensive ways to reduce energy loss through your windows or patio doors.

Window replacement can be very expensive, but with *Here's How: Windows,* you may find that you're able to save thousands of dollars doing it yourself, and giving your home an upgrade.

Window Styles

The following pages contain examples of some of the types of windows you may consider for your home. Your imagination may lead you to other options and combinations of options.

Casement windows pivot on hinges mounted on the side. They have a contemporary look and offer good ventilation. Whether your window has exposed or concealed sash locks, casements have a reputation for weather-tight construction.

Double-hung windows slide up and down and have a traditional appearance. The newer-style, spring-mounted operating mechanism is virtually trouble-free. The dividers (muntins) may divide individual panes of glass or snap on for decoration.

Bay windows consist of three parts: a central window, usually fixed, parallel to the existing wall, and two side windows (often casements or double-hungs), each set at a 30°, 45°, or 60° angle. The deep sill area makes a handy shelf space.

Bow windows have four or more units set at incremental angles to one another. The effect is a subtle, curved look. When large units are used, the bow window may become an extension of the room, even taking the place of a wall.

Garden windows bring the outside in by creating shelf space and letting in sunshine as well as fresh air. Many types are easy-to-install kits that fit into an existing window space. They can be added to any room in the home.

Sliding windows are inexpensive and require little maintenance, but they provide restricted ventilation since only half the window can be open at one time. However, that may be an acceptable tradeoff for a large, unobstructed view.

Awning windows pivot on hinges mounted at the top. Awning windows work well in combination with other windows, and because they provide ventilation without letting moisture in, they are a good choice in damp climates.

Fixed windows do not open, and they can be any size and shape used in any room. They may be flanked by other fixed windows or opening styles such as awning, casement, or double-hung.

Window groupings in an endless number of shapes and sizes may be used to dramatic effect in a home. They can become the focal point of a room, serving to highlight a spectacular view and let in lots of sunshine.

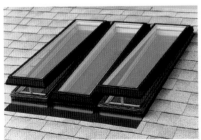

Skylights introduce extra light into rooms that have limited wall space. Skylights serve as solar collectors on sunny days, and those that also can be opened improve ventilation in the home.

Sliding patio doors offer good visibility and lighting. Because they slide on tracks and require no floor space for operation, they are a good choice for cramped spaces where swinging doors do not fit.

French doors open on hinges, so your room design must allow space for them to swing. Weather-tight models join indoor and outdoor living areas, while indoor models link two rooms.

1. New Window Sash

If you're looking to replace or improve old single- or double-hung windows, consider using sash-replacement kits. They can give you energy-efficient, maintenance-free windows without changing the outward appearance of your home or breaking your budget.

Unlike prime window replacement, which changes the entire window and frame, or pocket window replacement, in which a complete window unit is set into the existing frame, sash replacement uses the original window jambs, eliminating the need to alter exterior or interior walls or trim. Installing a sash-replacement kit involves little more than removing the old window stops and sashes and installing new vinyl jamb liners and wood or vinyl sash. And all of the work can be done from inside your home.

Most sash-replacement kits offer tilt features and other contemporary conveniences. Kits are available in vinyl, aluminum, or wood construction with various options for color and glazing, energy efficiency, security features, and noise reduction.

Nearly all major window manufacturers offer sash-replacement kits designed to fit their own windows. You can also order custom kits that are sized to your specific window dimensions. A good fit is essential to the performance of your new windows. Review the tips shown on the next page for measuring your existing windows, and follow the manufacturer's instructions for the best fit.

Tools & Materials ▶

Sill-bevel gauge
Flat pry bar
Scissors
Screwdriver
Nail set
Sash-replacement kit
Fiberglass insulation
1" galvanized roofing nails
Finish nails
Wood-finishing materials
Torpedo Level

Upgrade old, leaky windows with new, energy-efficient sash-replacement kits. Kits are available in a variety of styles to match your existing windows or to add a new decorative accent to your home. Most kits offer natural or painted interior surfaces and a choice of outdoor surface finishes.

How to Install a New Window Sash

Measure the width of the existing window at the top, middle, and bottom of the frame. Use the smallest measurement, then reduce the figure by ⅜". Measure the height of the existing window from the head jamb to the point where the outside edge of the bottom sash meets the sill. Reduce the figure by ⅜".
Note: Manufacturers' specifications for window sizing may vary.

Check for a straight, level, and plumb sill, side, and head jambs using a torpedo level. Measure the frame diagonally to check for square (if the diagonal measurements are equal, the frame is square). If the frame is not square, check with the sash-kit manufacturer: Most window kits can accommodate some deviation in frame dimensions.

Carefully remove the interior stops from the side jambs, using a putty knife or pry bar. Save the stops for reinstallation.

With the bottom sash down, cut the cord holding the sash, balancing weight on each side of the sash. Let the weights and cords fall into the weight pockets.

(continued)

Lift out the bottom sash. Remove the parting stops from the head and side jambs. (The parting stops are the strips of wood that separate the top and bottom sash.) Cut the sash cords for the top sash, then lift out the top sash. Remove the sash-cord pulleys. If possible, pull the weights from the weight pockets at the bottom of the side jambs, then fill the weight pockets with fiberglass insulation. Repair any parts of the jambs that are rotted or damaged.

Position the jamb-liner brackets, and fasten them to the jambs with 1" galvanized roofing nails. Place one bracket approximately 4" from the head jamb and one 4" from the sill. Leave $\frac{1}{16}$" clearance between the blind stop and the jamb-liner bracket. Install any remaining brackets, spacing them evenly along the jambs.

Position any gaskets or weatherstripping provided for the jamb liners. Carefully position each liner against its brackets and snap it into place. When both liners are installed, set the new parting stop into the groove of the existing head jamb, and fasten it with small finish nails. Install a vinyl sash stop in the interior track at the top of each liner to prevent the bottom sash from being opened too far.

Set the sash control mechanism, using a slotted screwdriver. Gripping the screwdriver firmly, slide down the mechanism until it is about 9" above the sill, then turn the screwdriver to lock the mechanism and prevent it from springing upward. The control mechanisms are spring-loaded—do not let them go until they are locked in place. Set the mechanism in each of the four sash channels.

Install the top sash into the jamb liners. Set the cam pivot on one side of the sash into the outside channel. Tilt the sash, and set the cam pivot on the other side of the sash. Make sure both pivots are set above the sash control mechanisms. Holding the sash level, tilt it up, depress the jamb liners on both sides, and set the sash in the vertical position in the jamb liners. Once the sash is in position, slide it down until the cam pivots contact the locking terminal assemblies.

Install the bottom sash into the jamb liners, setting it into the inside sash channels. When the bottom sash is set in the vertical position, slide it down until it engages the control mechanisms. Open and close both sash to make sure they operate properly.

Reinstall the stops that you removed in step 1. Fasten them with finish nails, using the old nail holes, or drill new pilot holes for the nails.

Check the tilt operation of the bottom sash to make sure the stops do not interfere. Remove the labels, and clean the windows. Paint or varnish the new sash as desired.

2. Framing & Installing Windows

Correct framing techniques will ensure ease of installation and keep your windows operating smoothly.

Many windows must be custom-ordered several weeks in advance. To save time, you can complete the interior framing before the window unit arrives, but be sure you have the exact dimensions of the window unit before building the frame. Do not remove the outside wall surface until you have the window and accessories and are ready to install them.

Follow the manufacturer's specifications for rough opening size when framing for a window. The listed opening is usually 1" wider and ½" taller than the actual dimensions of the window unit. The following pages show techniques for wood-frame houses with platform framing.

If your house has balloon framing where wall studs pass continuously from one floor to the next, use the method shown to install a header. Consult a professional to install a window on the second story of a balloon-framed house.

If your house has masonry walls or if you are installing polymer-coated windows, you may want to attach your window using masonry clips instead of nails.

Tools & Materials ▸

Tape measure	1" galvanized roofing
Pencil	nails
Combination square	Shims
Hammer	2× lumber
Level	⅛" plywood
Circular saw	Building paper
Handsaw	Drip edge
Pry bar	10d galvanized casing
Nippers	nails
Drill	8d casing nails
Reciprocating saw	Fiberglass insulation
Stapler	Paintable silicone caulk
Nail set	
Caulk gun	
10d common nails,	

How to Frame a Window Opening

Prepare the project site and remove the interior wall surfaces. Measure and mark the rough opening width on the sole plate. Mark the locations of the jack studs and king studs on the sole plate. Where practical, use the existing studs as king studs.

Measure and cut the king studs, as needed, to fit between the sole plate and the top plate. Position the king studs and toenail them to the sole plate with 10d nails.

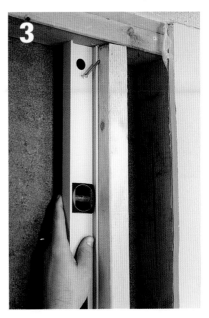

Check the king studs with a level to make sure they are plumb, then toenail them to the top plate with 10d nails.

Measuring from the floor, mark the top of the rough opening on one of the king studs. This line represents the bottom of the window header. For most windows, the recommended rough opening is ½" taller than the height of the window frame.

Measure and mark where the top of the window header will fit against the king studs. The header size depends on the distance between the king studs. Use a carpenter's level to extend the lines across the old studs to the opposite king stud.

Measure down from the header line and mark the double rough sill on the king stud. Use a carpenter's level to extend the lines across the old studs to the opposite king stud. Make temporary supports if removing more than one stud.

(continued)

7

Bottom of sill

Set a circular saw to its maximum blade depth, then cut through the old studs along the lines marking the bottom of the rough sill and along the lines marking the top of the header. Do not cut the king studs. On each stud, make an additional cut about 3" above the sill cut. Finish the cuts with a handsaw.

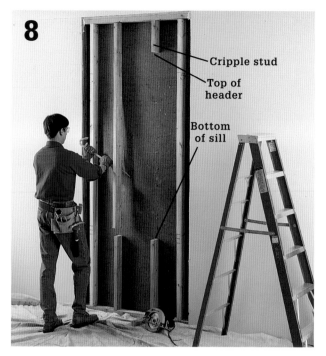

8

Cripple stud

Top of header

Bottom of sill

Knock out the 3" stud sections, then tear out the old studs inside the rough opening, using a pry bar. Clip away any exposed nails, using nippers. The remaining sections of the cut studs will serve as cripple studs for the window.

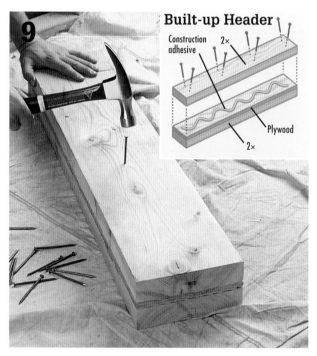

9

Built-up Header

Construction adhesive

2×

Plywood

2×

Build a header to fit between the king studs on top of the jack studs, using two pieces of 2× lumber sandwiched around ½" plywood.

10

Cut two jack studs to reach from the top of the sole plate to the bottom header lines on the king studs. Nail the jack studs to the king studs with 10d nails driven every 12". *Note: On a balloon-framed house the jack studs will reach to the sill plate.*

Position the header on the jack studs, using a hammer if necessary. Attach the header to the king studs, jack studs, and cripple studs, using 10d nails.

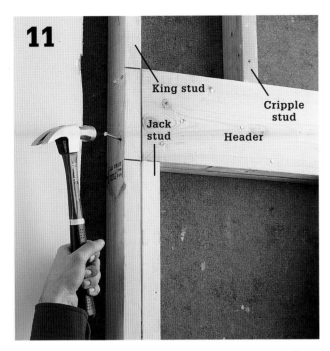

Build the rough sill to reach between the jack studs by nailing a pair of 2 × 4s together. Position the rough sill on the cripple studs, and nail it to the jack studs and cripple studs with 10d nails.

How to Install a Replacement Window with a Nailing Flange

Remove the existing window, and set the new window into the rough opening. Center it left to right, and shim beneath the sill to level it. On the exterior side, measure out from the window on all sides, and mark the siding for the width of the brick molding you'll install around the new window. Extend layout lines to mark where you'll cut the siding.

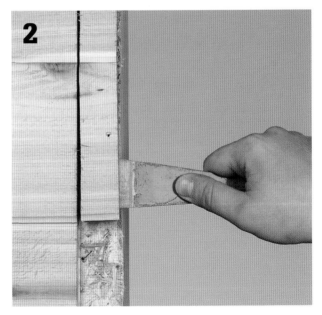

Remove exterior siding around the window area to expose the wall sheathing. Use a zip tool to separate vinyl siding for removal or use a pry bar and hammer to remove wood clapboard.

(continued)

Cover the sill and rough opening framing members with self-adhesive, rolled flashing. Apply additional strips of flashing behind the siding and up the sill flashing. Finish flashing with a strip along the header. The flashing should cover the front edges and sides of the opening members.

Apply a bead of silicone caulk around the back face of the window flange, then set it into the rough opening, centering it side-to-side in the opening. Tack the window in place by driving one roofing nail partway through the top flange. On the interior side, level and plumb the window, using shims to make any necessary adjustments.

Tack the window to the header at one end of the nailing flange, using a 1" galvanized roofing nail. Drive a roofing nail through the other top corner of the flange to hold the window in place, then secure the flange all around the window with more roofing nails. Apply strips of rolled, self-adhesive flashing to cover the window flanges. Start with a strip that covers the bottom flange, then cover the side flanges, overlapping the bottom flashing and extending 8 to 10" above the window. Complete the flashing with a strip along the top, overlapping the side flashing.

Install a piece of metal drip edge behind the siding and above the window. Secure it with silicone caulk only.

Cut and attach brick molding around the window, leaving a slight gap between the brick molding and the window frame. Use 8d galvanized casing nails driven into pilot holes to secure the brick molding to the rough framing. Miter the corner joints. Reinstall the siding in the window installation area, trimming as needed.

Use high-quality caulk to fill the gap between the brick molding and the siding. On the interior side, fill gaps between the window frame and surrounding framing with foam backer rod, low-expansion foam, or fiberglass insulation. Install the interior casing.

Tip Installation Variation: Masonry Clips ▸

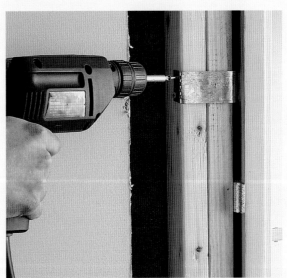

Use metal masonry clips when the brick molding on a window cannot be nailed because it rests against a masonry or brick surface. The masonry clips hook into precut grooves in the window jambs (above, left) and are attached to the jambs with screws. After the window unit is positioned in the rough opening, the masonry clips are bent around the framing members and anchored with screws (above, right). *Note: Masonry clips can also be used in ordinary lap siding installations if you want to avoid making nail holes in the smooth surface of the brick moldings. For example, windows that are precoated with polymer-based paint can be installed with masonry clips so that the brick moldings are not punctured with nails.*

How to Install a Round-Top Window

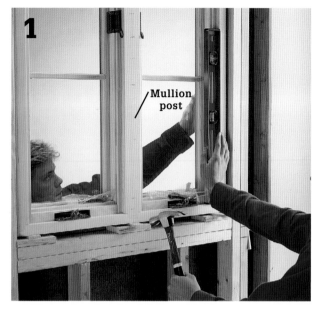

1

Remove the exterior wall surface, then test-fit the window, centering it in the rough opening. Support the window with wood blocks and shims placed under the side jambs and mullion post. Check to make sure the window is plumb and level, and adjust the shims, if necessary.

Mullion post

2

Trace the outline of the brick molding on the wood siding. Remove the window after finishing the outline. *Note: If you have vinyl or metal siding, you should have enlarged the outline to make room for the extra J-channel moldings required by these sidings.*

Tips for Framing a Round-top Window ▸

Create a template to help you mark the rough opening on the sheathing. Scribe the outline of the curved frame on cardboard, allowing an extra ½" for adjustments within the rough opening. A ¼ × 1¼" metal washer makes a good spacer for scribing the outline. Cut out the template along the scribed line.

Tape the template to the sheathing, with the top flush against the header. Use the template as a guide for attaching diagonal framing members across the top corners of the framed opening. The diagonal members should just touch the template. Outline the template on the sheathing as a guide for cutting the exterior wall surface.

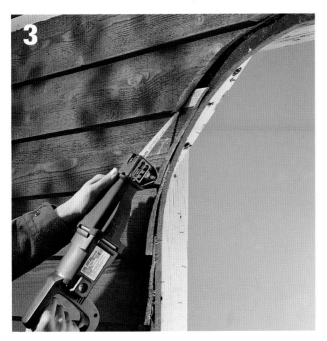

3

Cut the siding along the outline just down to the sheathing. For a round-top window, use a reciprocating saw held at a low angle. For straight cuts, use a circular saw adjusted so the blade cuts through only the siding. Use a sharp chisel to complete the cuts at the corners.

4

Cut 8"-wide strips of building paper and slide them between the siding and sheathing around the entire window opening. Bend the paper around the framing members and staple it in place. Work from the bottom up, so each piece overlaps the piece below. *Note: You can also use adhesive-backed, rolled flashing instead of building paper.*

5

Cut a length of drip edge to fit over the top of the window, then slide it between the siding and building paper. For round-top windows, use flexible vinyl drip edge; for rectangular windows, use rigid metal drip edge (inset).

6

Insert the window in the opening, and push the brick molding tight against the sheathing. Nail through the brick molding, as usual, to secure the window in the opening.

How to Frame a Window in a Gable Wall

Although most windows in a home are located in load-bearing exterior walls, standard attic windows are commonly located in gable walls, which often are non-loadbearing. Installing a window in a non-loadbearing gable wall is fairly simple and doesn't require a temporary support for the framing. Some gable walls, however, are load-bearing: A common sign is a heavy structural ridge beam that supports the rafters from underneath, rather than merely at the rafter ends. Hire a contractor to build window frames in load-bearing gable walls. If you aren't certain what type of wall you have, consult a professional.

A common problem with framing in a gable wall is that the positions of the floor joists may make it difficult to attach new studs to the wall's sole plate. One solution is to install an extra-long header and sill between two existing studs, positioning them at the precise heights for the rough opening. You can then adjust the width of the rough opening by installing vertical studs between the header and sill.

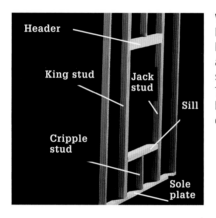

Window frames have full-length king studs, as well as jack studs that support the header. The sill defines the bottom of the rough opening.

Tools & Materials ▸

Circular saw
Handsaw
Plumb bob
T-bevel
4-ft. level
Combination square
Reciprocating saw

Framed window or door unit
2 × 4 lumber
16d, 10d, and 8d common nails
½"-thick plywood
Construction adhesive

Determine the rough opening width by measuring the window unit and adding 1". Add 3" to that dimension to get the distance between the king studs. Mark the locations of the king studs onto the sole plate of the gablewall.

Using a plumb bob, transfer the king-stud marks from the sole plate to the sloping top plates of the gable wall.

Cut the king studs to length, angle-cutting the top ends so they meet flush with the top plates. Fasten each king stud in place by toenailing the ends with three 8d nails.

Find the height of the rough opening by measuring the height of the window unit and adding ½". Measure up from where the finished floor height will be, and mark the top of the sill. Make a second mark for the bottom of the sill, 3" down from the top mark.

Measure up from the top sill mark, and mark the height of the rough opening (bottom of header). Make another mark 3½" up, to indicate the top of the header. Using a level, transfer all of these marks to the other king stud and to all intermediate studs.

Draw level cutting across the intermediate studs at the marks for the bottom of the sill and top of the header. Cut along the lines with a reciprocating saw, then remove the cutout portions. The remaining stud sections will serve as cripple studs.

Cut the jack to reach from the sole plate to the bottom header marks on the king studs. Nail the jack studs to the inside faces of the king studs using 10d common nails driven every 16".

Build a built-up header with 2 × 4s and plywood (page 14). Size it to fit snugly between king studs. Set header on top of jack studs. Nail through king studs into header with 16d nails, then toenail jack studs and cripple studs to header using 8d nails.

Build a sill to fit snugly between jack studs by nailing together two 2 × 4s. Position the sill at the top sill markings, and toenail it to the jack studs. Toenail the cripple studs to the sill. See pages 15 to 17 to install the window.

3. Garden Windows

Although often found in kitchens, a garden window is an attractive option for nearly any room in your home. Projecting out from the wall 16 to 24", garden windows add space to a room, making it feel larger. The glass roof and box-like design make them ideal growing environments for plants or display areas for collectibles. Garden windows also typically include front- or side-opening windows. These allow for ventilation and are usually available in either awning or casement style.

Home stores often stock garden windows in several common sizes. However, it may be difficult to locate a stock window that will fit in your existing window rough opening. In cases like this you must rebuild the rough opening to the proper size. It may be worth the added expense to custom-order your garden window to fit into the existing rough opening.

The large amount of glass in a garden window has a direct effect on the window's energy efficiency. When purchasing a garden window, as a minimum, look for double-pane glass with low-emissivity (low-E) coatings. More expensive super-efficient types of glass are available for severely cold climates.

Installation methods for garden windows vary by manufacturer. Some units include a nailing flange that attaches to the framing and holds the window against the house. Other models hang on a separate mounting frame that attaches to the outside of the house. In this project, the garden window has a built-in mounting sleeve that slides into the rough opening and is attached directly to the rough framing.

Tools & Materials ▸

Tape measure	Shims
Hammer	Exterior trim
Level	Building paper
Framing square	3" screws
Circular saw	Drip edge
Wood chisel	Construction adhesive
Stapler	4d siding nails
Drill and bits	8d galvanized casing
Caulking gun	nails
Utility knife	Interior trim
Garden window kit	Paintable silicone caulk
Wood strips	
2 × 4s	

A garden window's glass roof makes it an ideal sun spot for houseplants, and it can also help a room feel larger.

How to Install a Garden Window

1

Prepare the project site and remove the interior and exterior trim, then remove the existing window.

2

Check the rough opening measurements to verify the correct window sizing. The rough opening should be about ½" larger than the window height and width. If necessary, attach wood strips to the rough framing as spacers to bring the opening to the required size.

3

Use a level to check that the sill of the rough opening is level and the side jambs are plumb. Use a framing square to make sure each corner is square. The rough framing must be in good condition in order to support the weight of the garden window. If the framing is severely deteriorated or out of plumb or square, you may need to reframe the rough opening (pages 13 to 15).

4

Insert the garden window into the opening, pressing it tight against the framing. Support the unit with notched 2 × 4s under the bottom edge of the window until it has been fastened securely to the framing.

(continued)

5

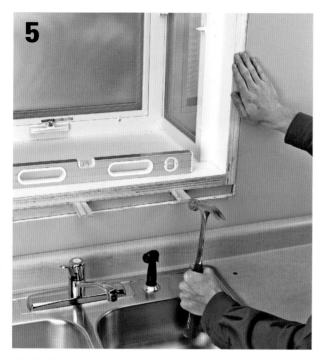

The inside edge of the window sleeve should be flush with the interior wall surface. Check the sill of the garden window for level. Shim beneath the lower side of the sill, if necessary, to make it level.

6

Once the garden window is in place and level, hold a piece of window trim in place along the exterior of the window and trace the outline onto the siding. Remove the window. Cut the siding down to the sheathing using a circular saw.

7

Install strips of building paper between siding and sheathing. Wrap them around the framing and staple them in place. On the sides, work from the bottom up so each piece overlaps the piece below. Reposition the window and reshim. Make sure the space between the window and the siding is equal to the width of the trim on all sides.

8

Drill countersunk pilot holes every 12" to 16" through the window sleeve into the rough header, jack studs, and sill.

9

Insert shims between the window sleeve and rough frame at each hole location along the top and sides to prevent bowing of the window frame. Fasten the window to the framing using 3" screws. Continue checking for level, plumb, and square as the screws are tightened.

10

Locate and mark the studs nearest the edges of the window using a stud finder. Cut two pieces of siding to fit behind the brackets, and tack them in place over the marked studs with 4d siding nails. Position the support brackets with the shorter side against the siding and the longer side beneath the window. Fasten the brackets to the window and the studs using the included screws.

11

Cut a piece of drip edge to length, apply construction adhesive to its top flange, and slide it under the siding above the window. Cut each trim piece to size. Position the trim and attach it using 8d galvanized casing nails driven through pilot holes. Seal the edges of the trim with a bead of paintable silicone caulk, approximately ⅜" wide.

12

Cut all protruding shims flush with the framing using a utility knife or handsaw. Insulate or caulk gaps between the window sleeve and the wall. Finish the installation by reinstalling the existing interior trim or installing new trim.

4. Bay Windows

Modern bay windows are preassembled for easy installation, but it will still take several days to complete an installation. Bay windows are large and heavy, and installing them requires special techniques.

Have at least one helper to assist you, and try to schedule the work when there's little chance of rain. Using prebuilt bay window accessories will speed your work (see next page).

A large bay window can weigh several hundred pounds, so it must be anchored securely to framing members in the wall and supported by braces attached to framing members below the window. Some window manufacturers include cable-support hardware that can be used instead of metal support braces.

Before purchasing a bay window unit, check with the local building department regarding the code requirements. Many local codes require large windows and low bay windows with window seats to be glazed with tempered glass for safety.

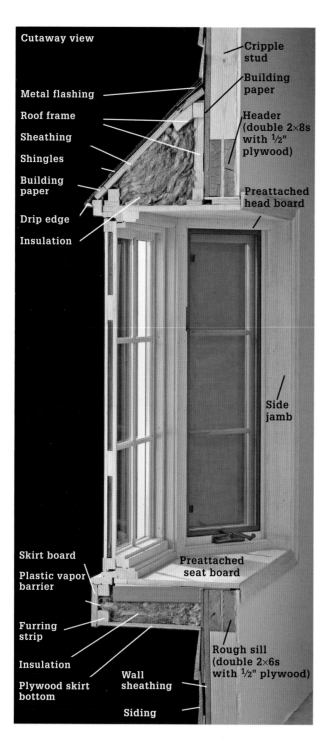

Cutaway view

Metal flashing
Roof frame
Sheathing
Shingles
Building paper
Drip edge
Insulation

Cripple stud
Building paper
Header (double 2×8s with ½" plywood)
Preattached head board

Side jamb

Skirt board
Plastic vapor barrier
Furring strip
Insulation
Plywood skirt bottom

Preattached seat board

Wall sheathing

Rough sill (double 2×6s with ½" plywood)

Siding

Tools & Materials ▸

Straightedge	3" and 2" galvanized
Circular saw	utility screws
Wood chisel	16d casing nails
Pry bar	Tapered wood shims
Drill	Building paper
Level	Fiberglass insulation
Nail set	6-mil polyethylene
Stapler	sheeting
Aviation snips	Drip edge
Roofing knife	1" roofing nails
Caulk gun	Step flashing
Utility knife	Shingles
T-bevel	Top flashing
Bay window unit	Roofing cement
Prebuilt roof frame	2 × 2 lumber
kit	5½" skirt boards
Metal support	¾" exterior-grade
brackets	plywood
2× lumber	Paintable silicone caulk
16d galvanized	
common nails	
16d and 8d	
galvanized casing	
nails	

Tips for Installing a Bay Window ▶

Use prebuilt accessories to ease installation of a bay window. Roof frames (A) come complete with sheathing (B), metal top flashing (C), and step flashing (D) and can be special-ordered at most home centers. You will have to specify the exact size of your window unit and the angle (pitch) you want for the roof. You can cover the roof inexpensively with building paper and shingles or order a copper or aluminum shell. Metal support braces (E) and skirt boards (F) can be ordered at your home center if not included with the window unit. Use two braces for bay windows up to 5 ft. wide and three braces for larger windows. Skirt boards are clad with aluminum or vinyl and can be cut to fit with a circular saw or miter saw.

Construct a bay window frame similar to that for a standard window (see pages 13 to 15) but use a built-up sill made from two 2 × 6s sandwiched around ½" plywood. Install extra jack studs under the sill ends to help carry the window's weight.

Build an enclosure above the bay window if the roof soffit overhangs the window. Build a 2 × 2 frame (top) to match the angles of the bay window, and attach the frame securely to the wall and overhanging soffit. Install a vapor barrier and insulation (page 34), then finish the enclosure so it matches the siding (bottom).

How to Install a Bay Window

Prepare the project site and remove interior wall surfaces, then frame the rough opening. Remove the exterior wall surfaces. Mark for removal a section of siding directly below the rough opening. The width of the marked area should equal that of the window unit and the height should equal that of the skirt board.

Set the blade on a circular saw just deep enough to cut through the siding, then cut along the outline. Stop just short of the corners to avoid damaging the siding outside the outline. Use a sharp chisel to complete the corner cuts. Remove the cut siding inside the outline.

Position the support braces along the rough sill within the widest part of the bay window and above the cripple stud locations. Add cripple studs to match the support brace locations, if necessary. Draw outlines of the braces on the top of the sill. Use a chisel or circular saw to notch the sill to a depth equal to the thickness of the top arm of the support braces.

Slide the support braces down between the siding and the sheathing. Pry the siding material away from the sheathing slightly to make room for the braces, if necessary. *Note: On stucco, you will need to chisel notches in the masonry surface to fit the support braces.*

5

16d nails

Attach the braces to the rough sill with galvanized 16d common nails. Drive 3" utility screws through the front of the braces and into the rough sill to prevent twisting.

6

Lift the bay window onto the support braces and slide it into the rough opening. Center the unit within the opening.

7

Check the window unit to make sure it is level. If necessary, drive shims under the low side to level the window. Temporarily brace the outside bottom edge of the unit with 2 × 4s to keep it from moving on the braces.

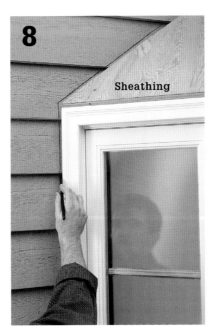

8

Sheathing

Set the roof frame on top of the window, with the sheathing loosely tacked in place. Trace the outline of the window and roof unit onto the siding. Leave a gap of about ½" around the roof unit to allow room for flashing and shingles.

9

Jack stud

Side jamb

Mark blocks flush with faces of studs

Shims

If the gap between the side jambs and jack studs is more than 1" wide, mark and cut wood blocks to bridge the gap (smaller gaps require no blocks). Leave a small space for inserting wood shims. Remove the window, then attach blocks every 12" along studs.

(continued)

Cut the siding just down to the sheathing along the outline using a circular saw. Stop just short of the corners, then use a wood chisel to complete the corner cuts. Remove the cut siding. Pry the remaining siding slightly away from the sheathing around the roof outline to allow for easy installation of the metal flashing. Cover the exposed sheathing with 8"-wide strips of building paper (step 4, page 19).

Set the bay window unit back on the braces, and slide it back into the rough opening until the brick moldings are tight against the sheathing. Insert wood shims between the outside end of the metal braces and the seat board (inset). Check the unit to make sure it is level, and adjust the shims, if necessary.

Anchor the window by drilling pilot holes and driving 16d casing nails through the brick molding and into the framing members. Space nails every 12", and use a nail set to drive the nail heads below the surface of the wood.

Drive wood shims into the spaces between the side jambs and the blocking or jack studs and between the headboard and header, spacing the shims every 12". Fill the spaces around the window with loosely packed fiberglass insulation. At each shim location, drive 16d casing nails through the jambs and shims and into the framing members. Cut off the shims flush with the framing members using a handsaw or utility knife. Use a nail set to drive the nail heads below the surface. If necessary, drill pilot holes to prevent splitting the wood.

14

Staple sheet plastic over the top of the window unit to serve as a vapor barrier. Trim the edges of the plastic around the top of the window using a utility knife.

15

Remove the sheathing pieces from the roof frame, then position the frame on top of the window unit. Attach the roof frame to the window and to the wall at stud locations using 3" utility screws.

16

Fill the empty space inside the roof frame with loosely packed fiberglass insulation. Screw the sheathing back onto the roof frame using 2" utility screws.

17

Staple asphalt building paper over the roof sheathing. Make sure each piece of building paper overlaps the one below by at least 5".

18

Cut drip edges with aviation snips, then attach them around the edge of the roof sheathing using roofing nails.

(continued)

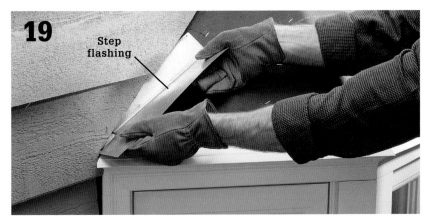

19

Step flashing

Cut and fit a piece of step flashing on each side of the roof frame. Adjust the flashing so it overhangs the drip edge by ¼". Flashings help guard against moisture damage.

20

Trim the end of the flashing to the same angle as the drip edge. Nail the flashing to the sheathing with roofing nails.

21

Cut 6"-wide strips of shingles for the starter row. Use roofing nails to attach the starter row shingles so they overhang the drip edge by about ½". Cut the shingles along the roof hips with a straightedge and a roofing knife.

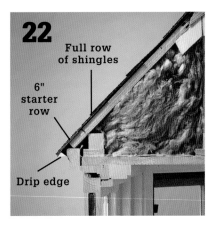

22

Full row of shingles

6" starter row

Drip edge

Nail a full row of shingles over the starter row, aligning the bottom edges with the bottom edge of the starter row. Make sure shingle notches are not aligned.

23

Second step flashing

Install another piece of step flashing on each side of the roof, overlapping the first piece of flashing by about 5".

24

Cut and install another row of full shingles. The bottom edges should overlap the tops of the notches on the previous row by ½". Attach the shingles with roofing nails driven just above the notches.

25 Continue installing alternate rows of step flashing and shingles to the top of the roof. Bend the last pieces of step flashing to fit over the roof hips.

26 When the roof sheathing is covered with shingles, install the top flashing. Cut and bend the ends over the roof hips, and attach it with roofing nails. Attach the remaining rows of shingles over the top flashing.

27 Find the height of the final row of shingles by measuring from the top of the roof to a point ½" below the top of the notches on the last installed shingle. Trim the shingles to fit.

28 Attach the final row of shingles with a thick bead of roofing cement—not nails. Press firmly to ensure a good bond.

29 Make ridge caps by cutting shingles into 1-ft.-long sections. Use a roofing knife to trim off the top corners of each piece, so the ridge caps will be narrower at the top than at the bottom.

30 Install the ridge caps over the roof hips, beginning at the bottom of the roof. Trim the bottom ridge caps to match the edges of the roof. Keep the same amount of overlap with each layer.

(continued)

31

At the top of the roof hips, use a roofing knife to cut the shingles to fit flush with the wall. Attach the shingles with roofing cement—do not use any nails.

32

Staple sheet plastic over the bottom of the window unit to serve as a vapor barrier. Trim the plastic around the bottom of the window.

33

Cut and attach a 2 × 2 skirt frame around the bottom of the bay window using 3" galvanized utility screws. Set the skirt frame back about 1" from the edges of the window.

34

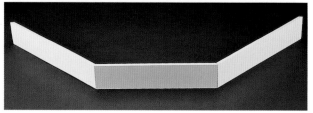

Cut skirt boards to match the shape of the bay window bottom, mitering the ends to ensure a tight fit. Test-fit the skirt board pieces to make sure they match the bay window bottom.

35

Cut a 2 × 2 furring strip for each skirt board. Miter the ends to the same angles as the skirt boards. Attach the furring strips to the back of the skirt boards, 1" from the bottom edges, using 2" galvanized utility screws.

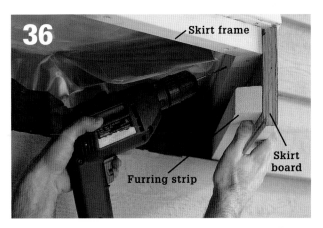

36

Skirt frame

Skirt board

Furring strip

Attach the skirt board pieces to the skirt frame. Drill ⅛" pilot holes every 6" through the back of the skirt frame and into the skirt boards, then attach the skirt boards with 2" galvanized utility screws.

37

Measure the space inside the skirt boards using a T-bevel to duplicate the angles. Cut a skirt bottom from ¾" exterior-grade plywood to fit this space.

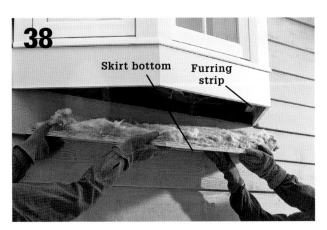

38

Skirt bottom   Furring strip

Lay fiberglass insulation on the skirt bottom. Position the skirt bottom against the furring strips and attach it by driving 2" galvanized utility screws every 6" through the bottom and into the furring strips.

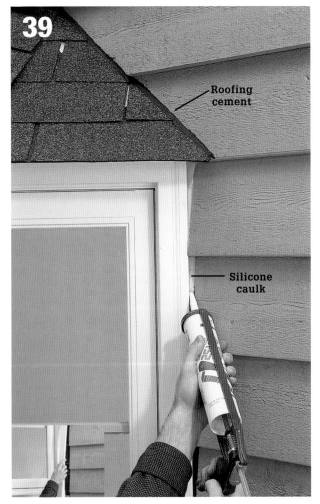

39

Roofing cement

Silicone caulk

Install any additional trim pieces (inset) specified by your window manufacturer using 8d galvanized casing nails. Seal the roof edges with roofing cement, and seal around the rest of the window with paintable silicone caulk.

5. Glass Block Windows

Glass block is a durable material that transmits light while reducing visibility, making it a perfect material for creating unique windows. Glass block windows are energy-efficient and work particularly well as accent windows or in rooms where privacy is desired, such as bathrooms.

Glass block is available in a wide variety of sizes, shapes, and patterns. It can be found, along with other necessary installation products, at specialty distributors or home centers.

Building with glass block is much like building with mortared brick, with two important differences. First, glass block must be supported by another structure and cannot function in a load-bearing capacity. Second, glass block cannot be cut, so take extra time to make sure the layout is accurate.

When installing a glass block window, the size of the rough opening is based on the size and number of blocks you are using. It is much easier to make an existing opening smaller to accommodate the glass block rather than make it larger, which requires reframing the rough opening. To determine the rough opening width, multiply the nominal width of the glass block by the number of blocks horizontally and add $\frac{1}{4}$". For the height, multiply the nominal height by the number of blocks vertically and add $\frac{1}{4}$".

Because of its weight, a glass block window requires a solid base. The framing members of the rough opening will need to be reinforced. Contact your local building department for requirements in your area.

Use $\frac{1}{4}$" plastic T-spacers between blocks to ensure consistent mortar joints and to support the weight of the block to prevent mortar from squeezing out before it sets. (T-spacers can be modified into L or flat shapes for use at corners and along the channel.) For best results, use premixed glass block mortar. This high-strength mortar is a little drier than regular brick mortar, because glass doesn't wick water out of the mortar as brick does.

Because there are many applications for glass block and installation techniques may vary, ask a glass block retailer or manufacturer about the best products and methods for your specific project.

Glass block windows provide exceptional durability, light transmission, and privacy. New installation products are also making these windows easier for the do-it-yourselfer to install.

Tools & Materials ▸

Tape measure	Caulk gun
Circular saw	2 × 4 lumber
Hammer	16d common nails
Utility knife	Glass block perimeter
Tin snips	channels
Drill	1" galvanized flat-head
Mixing box	screws
Trowel	Glass block mortar
4-ft. level	Glass blocks
Rubber mallet	$\frac{1}{4}$" T-spacers
Jointing tool	Expansion strips
Sponge	Silicone caulk
Nail set	Construction adhesive
Paintbrush	Mortar sealant

How to Install a Glass Block Window

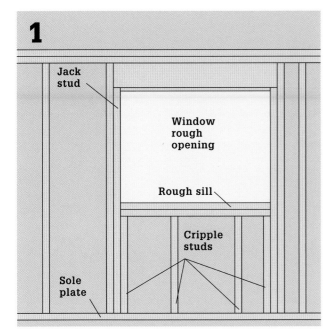

Measure the size of the rough opening and determine the size of the glass block window you will install (opposite page). Reinforce the rough opening framing by doubling the rough sill and installing additional cripple studs. Cut all pieces to size and fasten with 16d common nails.

Cut the perimeter channel to length for the sill and side jambs, mitering the ends at 45°. Align the front edge of the channel flush with the front edge of the exterior wall sheathing. Drill pilot holes every 12" through the channels (if not provided), and fasten the channels in place with 1" galvanized flat-head screws. *Note: Paint screw heads white to help conceal them.*

For the header, cut a channel to length, mitering the ends at 45°, then cut it in half lengthwise, using a utility knife. Align one-half of the channel flush with the exterior face of the sheathing, and fasten in place with 1" galvanized flat-head screws.

Set two blocks into the sill channel, one against each jamb—do not place mortar between blocks and channels. Place a ¼" flat spacer against the first block. Mix glass block mortar and liberally butter the leading edge of another block, then push it tight against the first block. Make sure the joint is filled with mortar.

(continued)

Lay the remainder of the first course, building from both jambs toward the center. Use flat spacers between blocks to maintain proper spacing. Plumb and level each block as you work, then also check the entire course for level. Tap blocks into place using the rubber handle of the trowel—do not use metal tools with glass block. Butter both sides of the final block in the course to install it.

At the top of the course, fill any depression at the top of each mortar joint with mortar and insert a ¼" T-spacer, then lay a ⅜" bed of mortar for the next course. Lay the blocks for each course, using T-spacers to maintain proper spacing. Check each block for level and plumb as you work.

Test the mortar as you work. When it can resist light finger pressure, remove the T-spacers (inset) and pack mortar into the voids, then tool the joints with a jointing tool. Remove excess mortar with a damp sponge or a bristle brush.

To ease block placement in the final course, trim the outer tabs off one side of the T-spacers using tin snips. Install the blocks of the final course. After the final block is installed, work in any mortar that has been forced out of the joints.

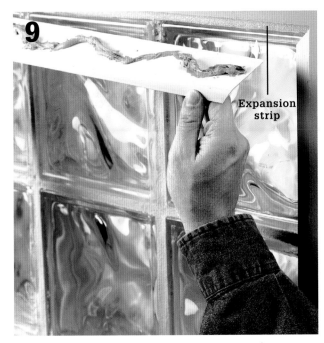

9

10

Expansion strip

Cut an expansion strip for the header 1½" wide and to length. Slide it between the top course of block and the header of the rough opening. Apply a bead of construction adhesive to the top edge of the remaining half of the header channel, and slide it between the expansion strip and header.

Clean the glass block thoroughly with a wet sponge, rinsing often. Allow the surface to dry, then remove cloudy residue with a clean, dry cloth. Caulk between glass block and channels and between channels and framing members before installing exterior trim. After brick molding is installed, allow the mortar to cure for two weeks. Apply sealant.

Variation: Glass Block Window Kits ▶

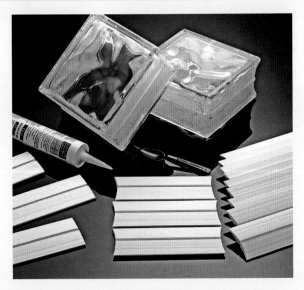

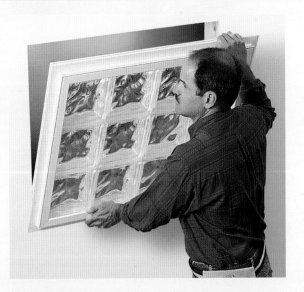

Some glass block window kits do not require mortar. Instead, the blocks are set into the perimeter channels and the joints are created using plastic spacer strips. Silicone caulk is then used to seal the joints.

Preassembled glass block windows are simple to install. These vinyl-clad units have a nailing flange around the frame, which allows them to be hung using the same installation techniques as for standard windows with a nailing flange (pages 15 to 17).

6. Skylights

Since skylights let in so much light, their sizing and placement are important considerations. A skylight that's too big can quickly overheat a space, especially in an attic. The same is true of using too many skylights in any one room. For that reason it's often best to position a skylight away from the day's brightest sun. You may want an operable skylight that opens and closes to vent warm air.

When a skylight is installed above an unfinished attic space, a special skylight shaft must be constructed to channel light directly to the room below.

Installing a skylight above finished space involves other considerations. First, the ceiling surface must be removed to expose the rafters. To remove wall and ceiling surfaces, see pages 46 to 49.

A skylight frame is similar to a standard window frame. It has a header and sill, like a window frame, but it has king rafters rather than king studs. Skylight frames also have trimmers that define the sides of the rough opening. Refer to the manufacturer's instructions to determine what size to make the opening for the skylight you select.

With standard rafter-frame roof construction, you can safely cut into one or two rafters as long as you permanently support the cut rafters, as shown in the following steps. If your skylight requires alteration of more than two rafters or if your roofing is made with unusually heavy material, such as clay tile or slate, consult an architect or engineer before starting the project.

Today's good-quality skylight units are unlikely to leak, but a skylight is only as leakproof as its installation. Follow the manufacturer's instructions, and install the flashing meticulously, as it will last a lot longer than any sealant.

Skylights can offer warmth in the winter, cooling ventilation in the summer, and a view of the sky or the treetops around your house during any season. And, of course, skylights provide natural light.

Tools & Materials ▸

4-ft. level	2", 1¼", and ¾"
Circular saw	roofing nails
Drill	Finish nails
Combination square	Fiberglass insulation
Reciprocating saw	½" wallboard
Pry bar	Twine
Chalk line	Wallboard screws
Stapler	6-mil polyethylene
Caulk gun	sheeting
Utility knife	Finishing materials
Aviation snips	
Plumb bob	
Jig saw	
Wallboard tools	
2 × lumber	
16d and 10d	
common nails	
1 × 4	
Building paper	
Roofing cement	
Skylight flashing	

How to Install a Skylight

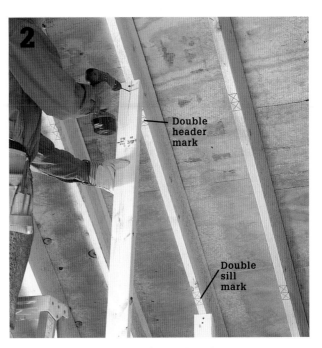

Use the first rafter on each side of the planned rough opening as a king rafter. Measure and mark where the double header and sill will fit against the king rafters. Then, use a level as a straightedge to extend the marks across the intermediate rafter.

Brace the intermediate rafter by installing two 2 × 4s between the rafter and the attic floor. Position the braces just above the header marks and just below the sill marks. Secure them temporarily to the rafter and subfloor (or joists) with screws.

Reinforce each king rafter by attaching a full-length "sister" rafter against its outside face. Cut sister rafters from the same size of lumber as existing rafters, matching lengths and end cuts exactly. Work each one into position, flush against the outside face of the king rafters, then nail the sisters to the kings with pairs of 10d common nails spaced 12" apart.

Use a combination square to transfer the sill and header marks across the face of the intermediate rafter, then cut along the outermost lines with a reciprocating saw. Do not cut into the roof sheathing. Carefully remove the cutout section with a pry bar. The remaining rafter portions will serve as cripple rafters.

(continued)

5

Build a double header and double sill to fit snugly between the king rafters, using 2× lumber that is the same size as the rafters. Nail the header pieces together using pairs of 10d nails spaced 6" apart.

6

Cripple rafter

Install the header and sill, anchoring them to the king rafters and cripple rafters with 16d common nails. Make sure the ends of the header and sill are aligned with the appropriate marks on the king rafters.

7

Trimmers

If your skylight unit is narrower than the opening between the king studs, measure and make marks for the trimmers: They should be centered in the opening and spaced according to the manufacturer's specifications. Cut the trimmers from the same 2× lumber used for the rest of the frame, and nail them in place with 10d common nails. Remove the 2 × 4 braces.

8

Mark the opening for the roof cutout by driving a screw through the sheathing at each corner of the frame. Then, tack a couple of scrap boards across the opening to prevent the roof cutout from falling and causing damage below.

9

From the roof, measure between the screws to make sure the rough opening dimensions are accurate. Snap chalk lines between the screws to mark the rough opening, then remove the screws.

10

Tack a straight 1 × 4 to the roof, aligned with the inside edge of one chalk line. Make sure the nail heads are flush with the surface of the board.

11

Cut through the shingles and sheathing along the chalk line using a circular saw and an old blade or a remodeling blade. Rest the saw foot on the 1 × 4, and use the edge of the board as a guide. Reposition the 1 × 4, and cut along the remaining lines. Remove the cutout roof section.

12

Remove the shingles around the rough opening with a flat pry bar, exposing at least 9" of building paper on all sides of the opening. Remove whole shingles rather than cutting them.

(continued)

Cut strips of building paper and slide them between the shingles and existing building paper. Wrap the paper so that it covers the faces of the framing members, and staple it in place.

Spread a 5"-wide layer of roofing cement around the roof opening. Set the skylight into the opening so that the nailing flange rests on the roof. Finally, adjust the unit so it sits squarely in the opening.

Nail through the flange and into the sheathing and framing members with 2" galvanized roofing nails spaced every 6". *Note: If skylight uses L-shaped brackets instead of a nailing flange, follow manufacturer's instructions.*

Patch in shingles up to the bottom edge of the skylight unit. Attach the shingles with 1¼" roofing nails driven just below the adhesive strip. If necessary, cut the shingles with a utility knife so they fit against the bottom of the skylight.

Spread roofing cement on the bottom edge of the sill flashing, then fit the flashing around the bottom of the unit. Attach flashing by driving ¾" galvanized roofing nails through the vertical side flange (near the top of the flashing) and into the skylight jambs.

Spread roofing cement on the bottom of a piece of step flashing, then slide flashing under the drip edge on one side of the skylight. Step flashing should overlap sill flashing by 5". Press the step flashing down to bond it. Repeat on the opposite side of the skylight.

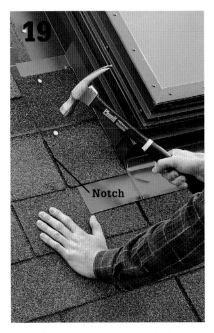

19

Patch in the next row of shingles on each side of the skylight, following the existing shingle pattern. Drive a 1¼" roofing nail through each shingle and the step flashing and into the sheathing. Drive additional nails just above the notches in the shingles.

20

Continue applying alternate rows of step flashing and shingles using roofing cement and roofing nails. Each piece of flashing should overlap the preceding piece by 5".

21

At the top of the skylight, cut and bend the last piece of step flashing on each side, so the vertical flange wraps around the corner of the skylight. Patch in the next row of shingles.

22

Spread roofing cement on the bottom of the head flashing to bond it to the roof. Place the flashing against the top of the skylight so the vertical flange fits under the drip edge and the horizontal flange fits under the shingles above the skylight.

23

Fill in the remaining shingles, cutting them to fit, if necessary. Attach the shingles with roofing nails driven just above the notches.

24

Apply a continuous bead of roofing cement along the joint between the shingles and the skylight. Finish the interior of the framed opening as desired.

How to Build a Skylight Shaft

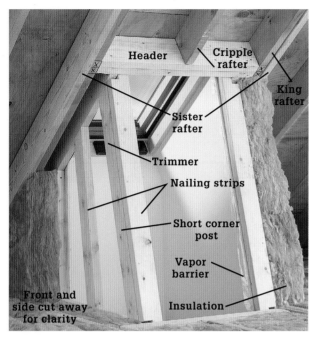

A skylight shaft is made with 2 × 4 lumber and wallboard and includes a vapor barrier and fiberglass insulation. You can build a straight shaft with four vertical sides or an angled shaft that has a longer frame at ceiling level and one or more sides set at an angle. Since the ceiling opening is larger, an angled shaft lets in more direct light than a straight shaft.

Remove any insulation in the area where the skylight will be located; turn off and reroute electrical circuits as necessary. Use a plumb bob as a guide to mark reference points on the ceiling surface, directly below the inside corners of the skylight frame.

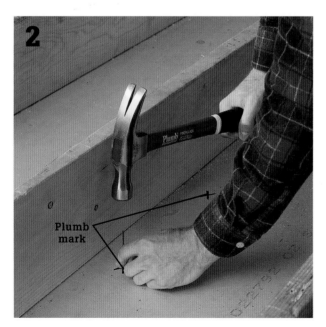

If you are installing a straight shaft, use the plumb marks made in step 1 to define the corners of the ceiling opening; drive a finish nail through the ceiling surface at each mark. If you are installing an angled shaft, measure out from the plumb marks and make new marks that define the corners of the ceiling opening; drive finish nails at the new marks.

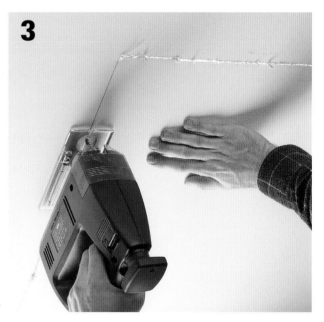

From the room below, mark cutting lines, then remove the ceiling surface.

Use the nearest joists on either side of the ceiling opening to serve as king joists. Measure and mark where the double header and double sill will fit against the king joists and where the outside edge of the header and sill will cross any intermediate joists.

If you will be removing a section of an intermediate joist, reinforce the king joists by nailing full-length "sister" joists to the outside faces of the king joists using 10d nails.

Install temporary supports below the project area to support the intermediate rafter on both sides of the opening. Use a combination square to extend cutting lines down the sides of the intermediate joist, then cut out the joist section with a reciprocating saw. Pry loose the cutout portion of the joist, being careful not to damage the ceiling surface.

Build a double header and double sill to span the distance between the king joists using 2× dimensional lumber the same size as the joists.

(continued)

Install the double header and double sill, anchoring them to the king joists and cripple joists with 10d nails. The inside edges of the header and sill should be aligned with the edge of the ceiling cutout.

Complete the ceiling opening by cutting and attaching trimmers, if required, along the sides of the ceiling cutout between the header and sill. Toenail the trimmers to the header and sill with 10d nails.

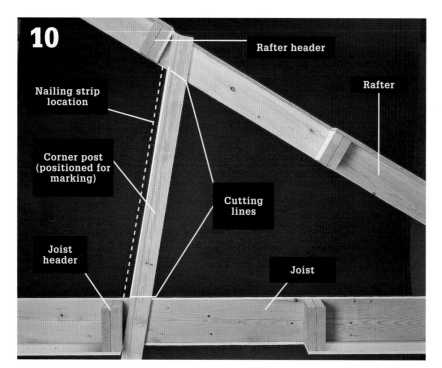

Install 2 × 4 corner posts for the skylight shaft. To measure for the posts, begin with a 2 × 4 that is long enough to reach from the top to the bottom of the shaft. Hold the 2 × 4 against the inside of the framed openings, so it is flush with the top of the rafter header and the bottom of the joist header (left photo). Mark cutting lines where the 2 × 4 meets the top of the joist or trimmer and the bottom of the rafter or trimmer (right photo). Cut along the lines, then toenail the posts to the top and bottom of the frame with 10d nails.

Attach a 2 × 4 nailing strip to the outside edge of each corner post to provide a nailing surface for attaching the wallboard. Notch the ends of the nailing strips to fit around the trimmers; a perfect fit is not necessary.

Install additional 2 × 4 nailing strips between the corner posts if the distances between posts are more than 24". Miter the top ends of the nailing strips to fit against the rafter trimmers.

Insulation removed for clarity

Wallboard and insulation removed for clarity

Wrap the skylight shaft with fiberglass insulation. Secure the insulation by wrapping twine around the shaft and insulation.

From inside the shaft, staple a plastic vapor barrier of 6-mil polyethylene sheeting over the insulation.

Finish the inside of the shaft, with wallboard. *Tip: To reflect light, paint the shaft interior with a light-colored, semigloss paint.*

7. Tubular Skylights

Any interior room can be brightened with a tubular skylight. Tubular skylights are quite energy-efficient and are relatively easy to install, with no complicated framing involved.

The design of tubular skylights varies among manufacturers, with some using solid plastic reflecting tubes and others using flexible tubing. Various diameters are also available. Measure the distance between the framing members in your attic before purchasing your skylight to be sure it will fit.

This project shows the installation of a tubular skylight on a sloped, asphalt-shingled roof. Consult the dealer or manufacturer for installation procedures on other roof types.

A tubular skylight is an economical way to introduce more sunlight into a room without embarking on a major framing project.

Tools & Materials ▸

Pencil	Reciprocating saw	Wire cutters	Stiff wire
Drill	Pry bar	Utility knife	2" roofing nails or
Tape measure	Screwdriver	Chalk	flashing screws
Wallboard saw	Hammer	Tubular skylight kit	Roofing cement

How to Install a Tubular Skylight

Drill a pilot hole through the ceiling at the approximate location for your skylight. Push a stiff wire up into the attic to help locate the hole. In the attic, make sure the space around the hole is clear of any insulation. Drill a second hole through the ceiling at the centerpoint between two joists.

Center the ceiling ring frame over the hole and trace around it with a pencil. Carefully cut along the pencil line with a wallboard saw or reciprocating saw. Save the wallboard ceiling cutout to use as your roof-hole pattern. Attach the ceiling frame ring around the hole with the included screws.

In the attic, choose the most direct route for the tubing to reach the roof. Find the center between the appropriate rafters and drive a nail up through the roof sheathing and shingles.

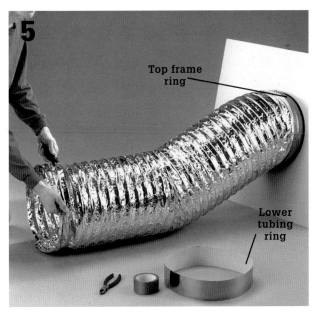

4

Use the wallboard ceiling cutout, centered over the nail hole, as a template for the roof opening. Trace the cutout onto the roof with chalk. Drill a starter hole to insert the reciprocating saw blade, then cut out the hole in the roof. Pry up the lower portion of the shingles above the hole. Remove any staples or nails around the hole edge.

5

Top frame ring

Lower tubing ring

Pull the tubing over the top frame ring. Bend the frame tabs out through the tubing, keeping two or three rings of the tubing wire above the tabs. Wrap the junction three times around with included PVC tape. Then, in the attic, measure from the roof to the ceiling. Stretch out the tubing and cut it to length with a utility knife and wire cutters. Pull the loose end of tubing over the lower ring and wrap it three times with PVC tape.

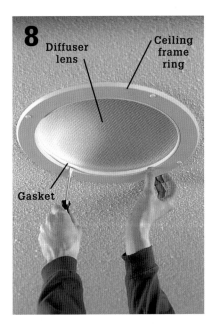

6

Lower the tubing through the roof hole and slide the flashing into place with the upper portion of the flashing underneath the existing shingles. This is easier with two people, one on the roof and one in the attic.

7

Secure the flashing to the roof with 2" roofing nails or flashing screws. Seal under the shingles and over all the nail heads with roofing cement. Attach the skylight dome and venting to the frame with the included screws.

8

Diffuser lens

Ceiling frame ring

Gasket

Pull the lower end of the tubing down through the ceiling hole. Attach the lower tubing ring to the ceiling frame ring and fasten it with screws. Attach the gasket to the diffuser lens and work the gasket around the perimeter of the ceiling frame. Repack any insulation around the tubing in the attic.

8. Basement Egress Windows

An egress window brings a pleasant source of natural light and ventilation to a dark, dank basement. More importantly, it can provide a life-saving means of escape in the event of a fire. Before you proceed with this project, check your local building code on egress windows. Contact your local building department to apply for the proper permits and to learn more about the code requirements for your area.

As long as the window opens wide enough to meet minimum standards for egress, the particular window style is really up to you. Casement windows are ideal, because they crank open quickly and provide unobstructed escape. A tall, double-hung window or wide sliding window can also work. Select a window with insulated glass and clad with vinyl or aluminum for durability; it will be subject to humidity and temperature fluctuations just like any other above-grade window in your home.

The second fundamental component of a basement egress window project is the subterranean escape well you install outside the foundation. There are several options to choose from: prefabricated well kits made of lightweight plastic that bolt together and are easy to install; corrugated metal wells are a lower-cost option; or, you can build a well from scratch using concrete, stone or landscape timber.

Installing an egress window involves four major steps: digging the well, cutting a new or larger window opening in the foundation, installing the window, and finally, installing the well. You'll save time and effort if you hire a backhoe operator to excavate the well. In most cases, you'll also need a large concrete saw (available at most rental stores) to cut the foundation wall.

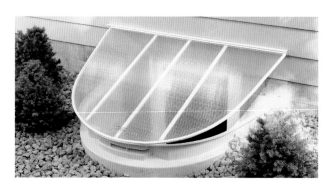

Replacing a small basement window with an egress window is a big job, but it is required if you want to convert part of a basement into livable space, especially a bedroom.

Tools & Materials ▸

Tape measure	Gloves
4-ft. level	Window well and
Stakes and string line	window
Shovel	Pea gravel
Colored masking	Plastic sheeting
tape	Self-tapping masonry
Hammer drill with	screws
½" dia. × 12- to	2× pressure-treated
16"-long masonry	lumber
bit	Shims
Concrete saw	Insulation materials
Hand maul	Concrete sleeve
Wide masonry chisel	anchors
Trowel, miter saw	
Drill/driver, hammer	
Caulk and caulk gun	

How to Install an Egress Window & Window Well

1

Lay out the border of the window well area with stakes and string. Plan the length and width of the excavation to be several feet larger than the window well's overall size to provide extra room for installation and adjustment.

2

Excavate the well to a depth 6 to 12" deeper than the well's overall height to allow room for drainage gravel. Make sure to have your local public utilities company inspect the well excavation area and okay it for digging before you start.

3

Measure and mark the foundation wall with brightly colored masking tape to establish the overall size of the window's rough opening (here, we're replacing an existing window). Be sure to take into account the window's rough opening dimensions, the thickness of the rough framing (usually 2x stock) and the width of the structural header you may need to build. Remember also that sill height must be within 44" of the floor. Remove existing wall coverings inside the layout area.

4

If the floor joists run perpendicular to your project wall, build a temporary support wall parallel to the foundation wall and 6 to 8 ft. from it. Staple sheet plastic to the wall and floor joists to form a work tent that will help control concrete dust.

(continued)

5

You'll need to cut through the foundation from both the inside and outside so the blocks will break cleanly. Drill a hole through the wall at each bottom corner with a hammer drill and long masonry bit to give you reference points for marking the outside cuts.

6

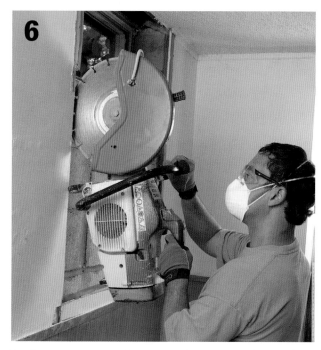

Equip a masonry cutting saw (or large angle grinder) with a diamond blade and set it for a ½" cut to score the blocks first, then reset the saw to full depth and make the final bottom and side cuts through the blocks. Wear a tight-fitting particle mask, ear and eye protection, and gloves for all of this cutting work; the saw will generate a tremendous amount of thick dust. Feed the saw slowly and steadily. Stop and rest periodically so the dust can settle.

7

Connect the holes you drilled previously with a level and plumb lines to mark the outside foundation wall for cutting. Measure the opening between the holes to make sure it is the correct size and that it is square. Score the cuts first, then make the full-depth cuts.

8

Strike the blocks with a hand maul to break or loosen the block sections. When all the blocks are removed, carefully chip away remaining debris with a cold chisel to create flat surfaces.

9

In concrete block walls, fill the hollow voids with broken pieces of block, then level and smooth the voids by trowelling on a fresh layer of quick-curing concrete. Flatten the surfaces, and allow the concrete to dry overnight.

10

If your project requires a new header above the new window, build it from pieces of 2× lumber sandwiching some ½" plywood and fastened together with construction adhesive and 10d nails. Slip it into place and tack it temporarily to the mudsill with 3½" deck screws driven toenail style.

11

Cut the sill plate for the window's rough frame from 2× treated lumber that's the same width as the thickness of the foundation wall. Fasten the sill to the foundation with ³⁄₁₆" × 3¼" countersunk masonry screws. Drill pilot holes for the screws first with a hammer drill.

12

Cut two pieces of treated lumber just slightly longer than the opening so they'll fit tightly between the new header and sill. Tap them into place with a maul. Adjust them for plumb and fasten them to the foundation with countersunk masonry screws or powder-actuated fasteners.

(continued)

13

Apply a thick bead of silicone caulk around the outside edges of the rough frame and set the window in its opening, seating the nailing flanges into the caulk. Shim the window so the frame is level and plumb. Test the action of the window to make sure the shims aren't bowing the frame.

14

Attach the window's nailing flanges to the rough frame with screws or nails, as specified by the manufacturer. Check the window action periodically as you fasten it to ensure that it still operates smoothly.

15

Seal gaps between the rough frame and the foundation with a bead of exterior silicone or polyurethane caulk. If the gaps are wider than 1/4", insert a piece of backer rod first, then cover it with caulk. On the interior, fill gaps around the window shims with strips of foam backer rod, fiberglass insulation, or a bead of minimally expanding spray foam. Do not distort the window frame.

16

Fill the well excavation with 6 to 12" of pea gravel. This will serve as the window's drain system. Follow the egress well kit instructions to determine the exact depth required; you may need to add more gravel so the top of the well will be above the new window. *Note: We added a drain down to the foundation's perimeter tile for improved drainage as well.*

17

Set the bottom section of the well into the hole, and position it evenly from left to right relative to the window. Adjust the gravel surface to level the well section carefully.

18

Stack the second well section on top of the first, and connect the two with the appropriate fasteners.

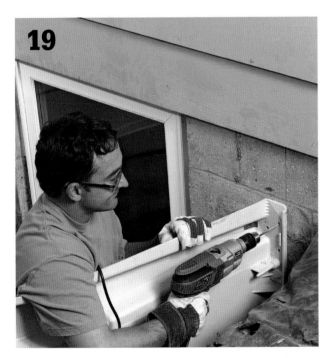

19

Fasten the window well sections to the foundation wall with concrete sleeve anchors driven into pre-bored pilot holes. You could also use masonry nails driven with a powder actuated nailer.

20

When all the well sections are assembled and secured, nail pieces of treated lumber trim around the window frame to hide the nailing flange. Complete the well installation by using excavated dirt to backfill around the outside of the well. Pack the soil with a tamper, creating a slope for good drainage. If you are installing a window well cover, set it in place and fasten it according to the manufacturer's instructions. The cover must be removable.

9. Patio Doors

For easy installation, buy a patio door with the door panels already mounted in a preassembled frame. Try to avoid patio doors sold with frame kits that require complicated assembly.

Because patio doors have very long bottom sills and top jambs, they are susceptible to bowing and warping. To avoid these problems, be very careful to install the patio door so it is level and plumb and to anchor the unit securely to framing members. Yearly caulking and touch-up painting helps prevent moisture from warping the jambs.

Tools & Materials ▸

Pencil	Nail set
Hammer	Shims
Circular saw	Drip edge
Handsaw	Building paper
Wood chisel	Silicone and latex caulk
Stapler	10d casing nails
Caulk gun	3" wood screws
Level	Sill nosing
Pry bar	Fiberglass insulation
Cordless screwdriver	Patio door kit
Drill and bits	

Patio doors offer the best qualities of both windows and doors—plenty of natural light, a great view, wide room access, and reasonable security.

If not included with the unit, screen doors can be ordered from most patio door manufacturers. Screen doors have spring-mounted rollers that fit into a narrow track on the outside of the patio door threshold.

Remove heavy glass panels if you must install the door without help. Reinstall the panels after the frame has been placed in the rough opening and nailed at opposite corners. To remove and install the panels, remove the stop rail found on the top jamb of the door unit.

Adjust the bottom rollers after installation is complete. Remove the coverplate on the adjusting screw, found on the inside edge of the bottom rail. Turn the screw in small increments until the door rolls smoothly along the track without binding when it is opened and closed.

Tips for Installing Hinged Patio Doors ▸

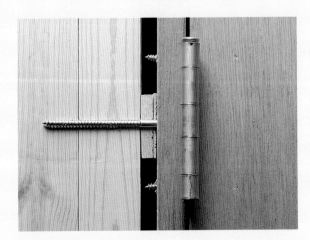

Provide extra support for door hinges by replacing the center mounting screw on each hinge with a 3" wood screw. These long screws extend through the side jambs and deep into the framing members.

Keep a uniform 1/8" gap between the door, side jambs, and top jamb to ensure that the door will swing freely without binding. Check this gap frequently as you shim around the door unit.

How to Install a Patio Door

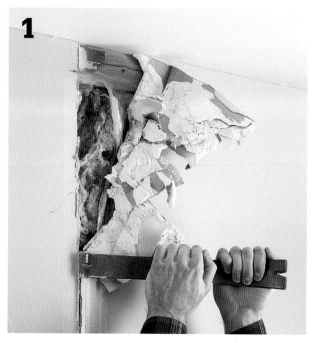

Prepare the work area and remove the interior wall surfaces, then frame the rough opening for the patio door. Remove the exterior surfaces inside the framed opening.

Test-fit the door unit, centering it in the rough opening. Check to make sure the door is plumb. If necessary, shim under the lower side jamb until the door is plumb and level. Have a helper hold the door in place while you adjust it.

Trace the outline of the brick molding onto the siding, then remove the door unit.

Cut the siding along the outline, just down to the sheathing using a circular saw. Stop just short of the corners to prevent damage to the remaining siding. Finish the cuts at the corners with a sharp wood chisel.

Drip edge

To provide an added moisture barrier, cut a piece of drip edge to fit the width of the rough opening, then slide it between the siding and the existing building paper at the top of the opening. Do not nail the drip edge.

6

Cut 8"-wide strips of building paper and slide them between the siding and sheathing. Bend the paper around the framing members and staple it in place. Each piece overlaps the piece below it.

7

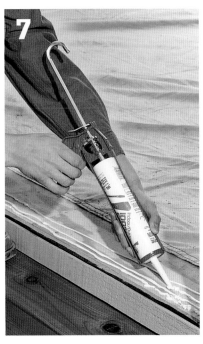

Apply several thick beads of silicone caulk to the subfloor at the bottom of the door opening.

8

Apply silicone caulk around the front edge of the framing members where the siding meets the building paper.

9

Use a pry bar to center the door in the rough opening so the brick molding is tight against the sheathing. Have a helper hold the door unit from outside.

10

Check the door threshold to make sure it is level. If necessary, shim under the lower side jamb until the patio door unit is level.

(continued)

If there are gaps between the threshold and subfloor, insert shims coated with caulk into the gaps, spaced every 6". Shims should be snug, but not so tight that they cause the threshold to bow. Clear off excess caulk immediately.

Place pairs of hardwood wedge shims together to form flat shims. Insert the shims every 12" into the gaps between the side jambs and the jack studs. For sliding doors, shim behind the strike plate for the door latch.

Insert shims every 12" into the gap between the top jamb and the header.

From outside, drive 10d casing nails, spaced every 12", through the brick molding and into the framing members. Use a nail set to drive the nail heads below the surface of the wood.

From inside, drive 10d casing nails through the door jambs and into the framing members at each shim location. Use a nail set to drive the nail heads below the surface of the wood.

16

Remove one of the screws and cut the shims flush with the stop block found in the center of the threshold. Replace the screw with a 3" wood screw driven into the subfloor as an anchor.

17

Cut off the shims flush with the face of the framing members using a handsaw. Fill gaps around the door jambs and beneath the threshold with loosely packed fiberglass insulation.

18

Reinforce and seal the edge of the threshold by installing sill nosing under the threshold and against the wall. Drill pilot holes and attach the sill nosing with 10d casing nails.

19

Make sure the drip edge is tight against the top brick molding, then apply paintable silicone caulk along the top of the drip edge and along the outside edge of the side brick moldings. Fill all exterior nail holes with caulk.

20

Caulk completely around the sill nosing, using your finger to press the caulk into any cracks. As soon as the caulk is dry, paint the sill nosing. Finish the door and install the lockset as directed by the manufacturer.

Stool & Apron Window Trim

Stool and apron trim brings a traditional look to a window, and it is most commonly used with double-hung styles. The stool serves as an interior sill; the apron (or the bottom casing) conceals the gap between the stool and the finished wall.

In many cases, such as with 2 × 6 walls, jamb extensions made from 1× finish-grade lumber need to be installed to bring the window jambs flush with the finished wall. Many window manufacturers also sell jamb extensions for their windows.

The stool is usually made from 1× finish-grade lumber, cut to fit the rough opening, with "horns" at each end extending along the wall for the side casings to butt against. The horns extend beyond the outer edge of the casing by the same amount that the front edge of the stool extends past the face of the casing, usually under 1".

If the edge of the stool is rounded, beveled, or otherwise decoratively routed, you can create a more finished appearance by returning the ends of the stool to hide the end grain. A pair of miter cuts at the rough horn will create the perfect cap piece for wrapping the grain of the front edge of the stool around the horn. The same can be done for an apron cut from a molded casing.

When installing these trim components, use a pneumatic nailer—you don't want to spend all that time shimming the jambs perfectly only to knock them out of position with one bad swing of a hammer.

As with any trim project, tight joints are the secret to a successful stool and apron trim job. Take your time to ensure all the pieces fit tightly.

Tip ▶

"Back cut" the ends of casing pieces where needed to help create tight joints using a sharp utility knife.

Tools & Materials ▶

Tape measure
Straightedge
Circular saw or
    jigsaw
Handsaw
Plane or rasp
Drill
Hammer
Pneumatic nailer
    (optional)
1× finish lumber
Casing

Wood shims
4d, 6d, and 8d finish
    nails

How to Install Stool & Apron Window Trim

Cut the stool to length, with several inches at each end for creating the horn returns. With the stool centered at the window and tight against the wallboard, shim it to its finished height. At each corner, measure the distance between the window frame and the stool, then mark that dimension on the stool.

Open a compass so it touches the wall and the tip of the rough opening mark on the stool, then scribe the plane of the wall onto the stool to complete the cutting line for the horn.

Cut out the notches for the horn using a jigsaw or a sharp handsaw. Test-fit the stool, making any minor adjustments with a plane or a rasp to fit it tightly to the window and the walls.

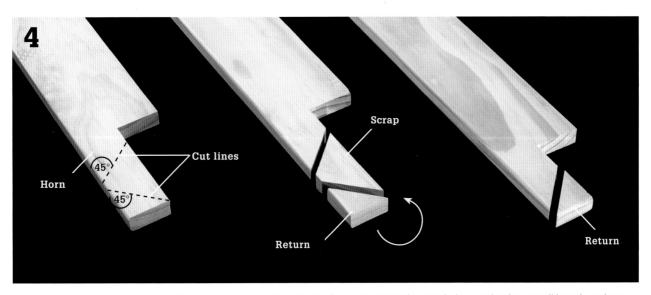

To create a return at the horn of the stool, miter-cut the return pieces at 45° angles. Mark the stool at its overall length and cut it to size with 45° miter cuts. Glue the return to the mitered end of the horn so the grain wraps around the corner. *Note: Use this technique to create the returns on the apron (step 13, page 67), but make the cuts with the apron held on-edge, rather than flat.*

(continued)

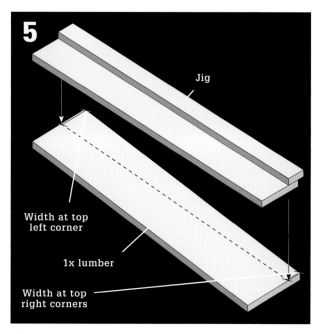

5

Jig

Width at top
left corner

1x lumber

Width at top
right corners

Where extensions are needed, cut the head extension to its finished length—the distance between the window side jambs plus the thickness of both side extensions (typically 1× stock). For the width, measure the distance between the window jamb and the finished wall at each corner, then mark the measurements on the ends of the extension. Use a straightedge to draw a reference line connecting the points. Build a simple cutting jig, as shown.

6

Clamp the jig on the reference line, then rip the extension to width using a circular saw; keep the baseplate tight against the jig and move the saw smoothly through the board. Reposition the clamp when you near the end of the cut. Cut both side extensions to length and width, using the same technique as for the head extension (step 5).

7

Build a box frame with the extensions and stool using 6d finish nails and a pneumatic nailer. Measure to make sure the box has the same dimensions as the window jambs. Drive nails through the top of the head extension into the side extensions and through the bottom of the stool into the side extensions.

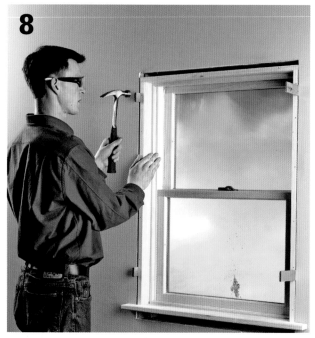

8

Apply wood glue to the back edge of the frame, then position it against the front edge of the window jambs. Use wood shims to adjust the frame, making sure the pieces are flush with the window jambs. Fasten the frame at each shim location using 8d finish nails driven through pilot holes. Loosely pack insulation between the framing members and extensions.

On the edge of each extension, mark a ¼" reveal at the corners, the middle, and the stool. Place a length of casing along the head extension, aligned with the reveal marks at the corners. Mark where the reveal marks intersect, then make 45° miter cuts at each point. Reposition the casing at the head extension and attach using 4d finish nails at the extensions and 6d finish nails at the framing members.

Cut the side casings to rough length, leaving the ends slightly long for final trimming. Miter one end at 45°. With the pointed end on the stool, mark the height of the side casing at the top edge of the head casing.

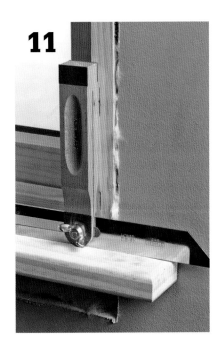

To get a tight fit for the side casings, align one side of a T-bevel with the reveal, mark the side extension, and position the other side flush against the horn. Transfer the angle from the T-bevel to the end of the casing, and cut the casing to length.

Test-fit the casings, making any final adjustments with a plane or rasp. Fasten the casing with 4d finish nails at the extensions and 6d finish nails at framing members.

Cut apron to length, leaving a few inches at each end for creating the returns (step 4, page 65). Position the apron tight against the bottom edge of the stool, then attach it using 6d finish nails driven every 12".

Basement Window Trim

Basement windows bring much-needed sunlight into dark areas, but even in finished basements they often get ignored on the trim front. This is partly because most basement foundation walls are at least 8" thick, and often a lot thicker. Add a furred-out wall and the window starts to look more like a tunnel with a pane of glass at the end. But with some well-designed and well-executed trim carpentry, you can turn the depth disadvantage into a positive.

A basement window opening may be finished with wallboard, but the easiest way to trim one is by making extra-wide custom jambs that extend from the inside face of the window frame to the interior wall surface. Because of the extra width, plywood stock is a good choice for the custom jambs. The project shown here is created with veneer-core plywood with oak veneer surface. The jamb members are fastened together into a nice square frame using rabbet joints at the corner. The frame is scribed and installed as a single unit and then trimmed out with oak casing. The casing is applied flush with the inside edges of the frame opening. If you prefer to have a reveal edge around the interior edge of the casing, you will need to add a solid hardwood strip to the edge of the frame so the plies of the plywood are not visible.

Tools & Materials ▸

Pencil	Finish-grade ¾" oak
Tape measure	plywood
Table saw, drill with	Spray-foam insulation
bits	1¼" composite or cedar
2-ft level	wood shims
Framing square	2" finish nails
Utility knife	1⅝" drywall screws
Straightedge	Carpenter's glue

Because they are set into thick foundation walls, basement windows present a bit of a trimming challenge. But the thickness of the foundation wall also lets you create a handy ledge that's deep enough to hold potted plants or even sunning cats.

How to Trim a Basement Window

Check to make sure the window frame and surrounding area are dry and free of rot, mold, or damage. At all four corners of the basement window, measure from the inside edges of the window frame to the wall surface. Add 1" to the longest of these measurements.

Set your table saw to make a rip cut to the width arrived at in step 1. If you don't have a table saw, set up a circular saw and straightedge cutting guide to cut strips to this length. With a fine-tooth panel-cutting blade, rip enough plywood strips to make the four jamb frame components.

Cross-cut the plywood strips to correct lengths. In our case, we designed the jamb frame to be the exact same outside dimensions as the window frame, since there was some space between the jamb frame and the rough opening.

Cut **³⁄₈"-deep × ³⁄₄"-wide rabbets** at each end of the head jamb and the sill jamb. A router table is the best tool for this job, but you may use a table saw or handsaws and chisels. Inspect the jambs first and cut the rabbets in whichever face is in better condition. To ensure uniformity, we ganged the two jambs together (they're the same length). It's also a good idea to include backer boards to prevent tear-out.

(continued)

Glue and clamp the frame parts together, making sure to clamp near each end from both directions. Set a carpenter's square inside the frame and check it to make sure it's square.

Before the glue sets, carefully drill three perpendicular pilot holes, countersunk, through the rabbeted workpieces and into the side jambs at each corner. Space the pilot holes evenly, keeping the end ones at least 3/4" in from the end. Drive a 1⅝" drywall screw into each pilot hole, taking care not to overdrive. Double-check each corner for square as you work, adjusting the clamps if needed.

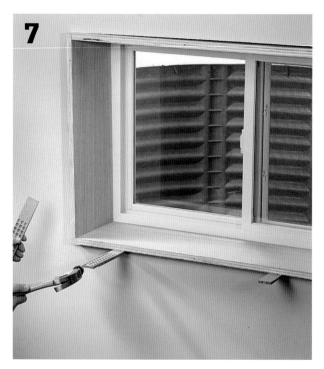

Let the glue dry for at least one hour (overnight is better), then remove the clamps and set the frame in the window opening. Adjust the frame so it is centered and level in the opening and the exterior-side edges fit flush against the window frame.

Taking care not to disturb the frame's position (rest a heavy tool on the sill to hold it in place if you wish), press a steel rule against the wall surface and mark trimming points at the point where the rule meets the jambs at each side of all four frame corners using a sharp pencil.

Remove the frame and clamp it on a flat work surface. Use a straightedge to connect the scribe marks at the ends of each jamb frame side. Set the cutting depth of your circular saw to just a small fraction over ¾". Clamp a straightedge guide to the frame so the saw blade will follow the cutting line and trim each frame side in succession. (The advantage of using a circular saw here is that any tear-out from the blade will be on the nonvisible faces of the frame.)

Replace the frame in the window opening in the same orientation as when you scribed it and install shims until it is level and centered in the opening. Drive a few finish nails through the side jambs into the rough frame. Also drive a few nails through the sill jamb. Most trim carpenters do not drive nails into the head jamb.

Insulate between the jamb frame and the rough frame with spray-in polyurethane foam. Look for minimal-expanding foam labeled "window and door" and don't spray in too much. Let the foam dry for a half hour or so and then trim off the excess with a utility knife. *Tip: Protect the wood surfaces near the edges with wide strips of masking tape.*

Remove the masking tape and clean up the mess from the foam (there is always some). Install case molding. We used picture-frame techniques to install fairly simple oak casing.

12. Replacing Broken Window Glass

For people who live in new, well-made houses, the windows from the ground to the ridge are bound to be double-glazed units that perform with commendable energy efficiency. This is a good thing, mostly. But these hi-tech units can break just like their older single-pane siblings. People who live in older houses have it better. Their single pane sash and storm windows are easier to repair. If you have just one pane to replace, most people can finish up the job in a couple of hours. Usually the hardest part of this chore is working off a ladder. You'll need one to remove the storm windows to fix a regular sash because the repair needs to be made on the outside of the window.

Tools & Materials ▸

Linseed oil
Heat gun
Glazing compound
Paint to match
Tape measure
Heavy leather gloves
Glazier's points

Glass pane
Razor blade paint
  scraper
Needlenose pliers
Putty knife
Paintbrush

Replacing a broken glass pane isn't nearly as common an occurrence today as it was a decade or two ago, before most homes had double-pane windows. But it's still a great skill to have for owners of older homes.

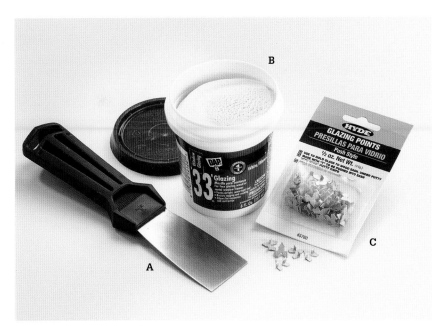

A clean putty knife (A), glazing compound (B,) and a package of glazier's points (C) are essential tools and materials for replacing window glass.

Tool Tip ▸

One way to be sure your glass supplier will cut your new glass panes accurately is if you provide a cardboard template that matches the pane size you need. Take this with you when ordering the glass.

Each glass pane in a typical wood sash is held in place in pockets on the muntins that form the sash and on the outside by glazing compound. This compound is a soft, caulk-like material when it's installed. But it hardens over time to form a durable seal that keeps the glass in the frame and the water out. If you wiggle the pieces of broken glass in and out, this will loosen the compound and you can pull the shards out.

How to Fix a Broken Windowpane

Wearing heavy leather gloves, remove the broken pieces of glass. Then, soften the old glazing compound using a heat gun or a hair dryer. Don't hold the heat gun too long in one place because it can be hot enough to scorch the wood or crack adjacent panes of glass.

Once a section of compound is soft, remove it using a putty knife. Work carefully to avoid gouging the wood frame. If a section is difficult to scrape clean, reheat it with the heat gun. Soft compound is always easy to remove.

Once the wood opening is scraped clean, seal the wood with a coat of linseed oil or primer. If the wood isn't sealed, the dry surface will draw too much moisture from the glazing compound and reduce its effectiveness.

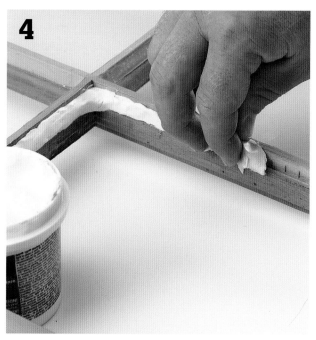

Apply a thin bed of glazing compound to the wood frame opening and smooth it in place with your thumb.

Press the new pane into the opening, making sure to achieve a tight seal with the compound on all sides. Wiggle the pane from side to side and up and down until the pane is seated. There will be some squeeze-out, but do not press all the compound out.

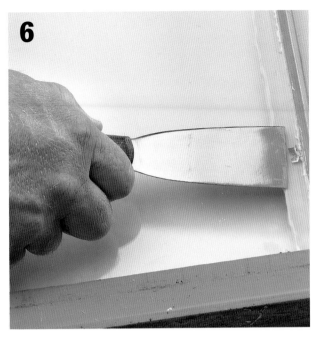

Drive glazier's points into the wood frame to hold the pane in place. Use the tip of a putty knife to slide the point against the surface of the glass. Install at least 2 points on each side of the pane.

Make a rope of compound (about ½" dia.) by rolling it between your hands. Then press it against the pane and the wood frame. Smooth it in place by drawing a putty knife, held at a 45° angle, across its surface. Scrape off excess.

Allow the glazing compound at least one week to dry completely. Then prime and paint it to match the rest of the sash. Be sure to spread the paint over the joint between the compound and the glass. This will seal the joint completely. When the paint is dry, scrape off the extra with a razor blade paint scraper.

13. Improving Window Operation

Many of us have experienced difficulty with opening windows due to swelled wood or painted channels. Almost as frequent, windows won't stay open because of a broken sash cord or chain. To avoid difficulties with windows, regular maintenance is crucial. Double-hung windows with spring-loaded sash tracks require cleaning and an occasional adjustment of the springs in (or behind) the tracks. Casement windows are often faulty at the crank mechanisms. If cleaning doesn't fix the problem, the crank mechanism must be replaced. For storm windows, the window track must be clean, and greaseless lubricant must be applied each time the windows and screens are removed.

Tools & Materials ▸

Screwdrivers	Toothbrush
Paint zipper or utility knife	Paint solvent
	Rags
Hammer	Sash cord
Vacuum	Lubricant
Small pry bar	Wax candle
Scissors	String
Stiff brush	All-purpose grease

Windows endure temperature extremes, house setting, and all sorts of wear and tear. Sooner or later you'll need to perform a bit of maintenance to keep them working properly.

How to Adjust Windows

Spring-loaded windows have an adjustment screw on the track insert. Adjust both sides until the window is balanced and opens and closes smoothly.

Spring-lift windows operate with the help of a spring-loaded lift rod inside a metal tube. Adjust them by unscrewing the top end of the tube from the jamb, then twisting the tube to change the spring tension: clockwise for more lifting power; counterclockwise for less. Maintain a tight grip on the tube at all times to keep it from unwinding.

Tips for Freeing Sticking Windows ▶

Cut the paint film if the window is painted shut. Insert a paint zipper or utility knife between the window stop and the sash, and slide it down to break the seal.

Place a block of scrap wood against the window sash. Tap lightly with a hammer to free the window.

Clean the tracks on sliding windows and doors with a hand vacuum and a toothbrush. Dirt buildup is common on storm window tracks.

Clean weatherstrips by spraying with a cleaner and wiping away dirt. Use paint solvent to remove paint that may bind windows. Then apply a small amount of lubricant to prevent sticking.

Lubricate wood window channels by rubbing them with a white candle, then open and close the window a few times. Do not use liquid lubricants on wood windows.

How to Replace Broken Sash Cords

1

Cut any paint seal between the window frame and stops with a utility knife or paint zipper. Pry the stops away from the frame, or remove the molding screws.

2

Bend the stops out from the center to remove them from the frame. Remove any weatherstripping that's in the way.

3

Slide out the lower window sash. Pull knotted or nailed cords from holes in the sides of the sash (see step 9).

4

Pry out or unscrew the weight pocket cover in the lower end of the window channel. Pull the weight from the pocket, and cut the old sash cord from the weight.

5

Tie one end of a piece of string to a nail and the other end to the new sash cord. Run the nail over the pulley and let it drop into the weight pocket. Retrieve the nail and string through the pocket.

6

Pull on the string to run the new sash cord over the pulley and through the weight pocket. Make sure the new cord runs smoothly over the pulley.

7

Attach the end of the sash cord to the weight using a tight double knot. Set the weight in the pocket. Pull on the cord until the weight touches the pulley.

8

Rest the bottom sash on the sill. Hold the sash cord against the side of the sash, and cut enough cord to reach 3" past the hole in the side of the sash.

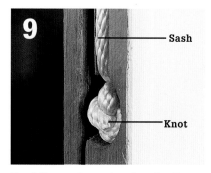

9

Knot the sash cord and wedge the knot into the hole in the sash. Replace the pocket cover. Slide the window and any weatherstripping into the frame, then attach the stops in the original positions.

How to Clean & Lubricate a Casement Window Crank

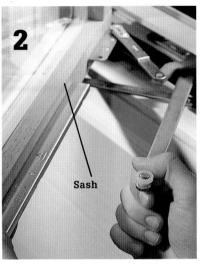

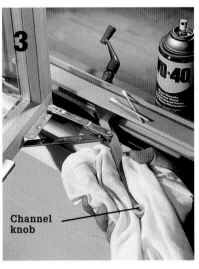

If a casement window is hard to crank, clean the accessible parts. Open the window until the roller at the end of the extension arm is aligned with the access slot in the window track.

Disengage the extension arm by pulling it down and out of the track. Clean the track with a stiff brush, and wipe the pivoting arms and hinges with a rag.

Lubricate the track and hinges with spray lubricant or household oil. Wipe off excess lubricant with a cloth, then reattach the extension arm. If that doesn't solve the problem, repair or replace the crank assembly (below).

How to Repair a Casement Window Crank Assembly

Disengage the extension arm from the window track, then remove the molding or cap concealing the crank mechanism. Unhinge any pivot arms connected to the window.

Remove the screws securing the crank assembly, then remove the assembly and clean it thoroughly. If the gears are badly worn, replace the assembly. Check a home center or call the manufacturer for new parts. Note which way the window opens—to the right or left—when ordering replacement parts.

Apply an all-purpose grease to the gears, and reinstall the assembly. Connect the pivot arms, and attach the extension arm to the window. Test the window operation before installing the cap and molding.

14. Replacing Insulated Glass Units (IGUs)

If you live in a newer home or have had your windows replaced at some point, chances are your windows contain double-pane, insulating glass units (IGU). IGU windows are much more energy efficient than the old, single-pane styles, but they aren't immune to the usual breakage calamities that affect glass. A more common problem with IGU windows, however, is leaky seals that can cause the glass to look foggy or etched.

The difficulty of changing an IGU depends on the window's design. IGUs are self-contained and fit inside the sash in one of two ways. Some window sash can be disassembled into sections. A gasket surrounds the IGU and fits into grooves in the sash members. If your sash has a screw at each corner, it may be this style, and it's easy for a do-it-yourselfer to repair. If there are no corner screws, chances are the sash is permanently assembled. With this style, the IGU is held in place with stop moldings and either specialized sealing tape or caulk. The stop moldings are attached to one side of the sash. On wood windows, look for filled nail holes in the trim area next to the glass; the putty hides the brads that hold the stop moldings in place. On vinyl or aluminum windows, the molding strips fit into channels in the sash frame. To locate the moldings on the sash, look for a slight color mismatch between the strips and the sash or tiny gaps around their edges that indicate these pieces are removable.

Tools & Materials ▸

Hammer
Screwdriver or drill/
  driver
Thin-blade putty
  knives
Small paint scraper
Scrap blocks

Neutral-cure silicone
  caulk
Replacement stop
  moldings
IGU gaskets or setting
  tape
Pneumatic brad nails,
  as required

Insulating glass units (IGUs) contain a pair of glass panes that trap inert gas between them to increase efficiency. Repairing a broken IGU is considerably harder than replacing a single pane, but it can be done.

Replacement Parts ▸

Before you attempt to replace a leaky IGU, remove the sash and take it to a window repair shop to seek an expert's advice. You'll need to have the shop take measurements for the replacement IGU anyway, and they can supply you with new gaskets, stop moldings, or specialized setting tape that might be required for the job. A window shop can also determine how old the window is. If the seal has failed and the window is less than 10 years old, the manufacturer's warranty may still be in effect.

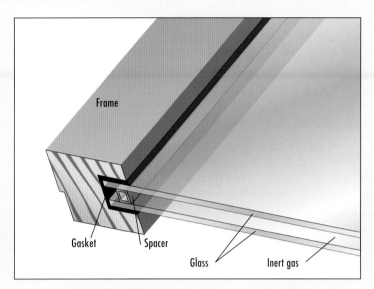

Some IGUs are made with wood frames that screw together, which presents a relatively easy fix for the DIYer. The new IGU is simply wrapped in a rubber gasket and reinstalled in the partially disassembled wood frame.

How to Replace an IGU in a Screw-type Sash

Use a screwdriver or drill/driver to remove two screws on the opposite corners of the sash frame. You can dismantle the frame into two L-shaped sections, which will make reassembly easier.

Pull the frame sections apart to remove the IGU. You may need to use a hammer to gently tap against a block of scrap wood to open the frame.

Peel the gasket off the old IGU. If it's undamaged, fit it around the new IGU, then slide the IGU in place between the sash sections. Reinstall the corner screws.

How to Replace an IGU in a Fixed-sash Frame

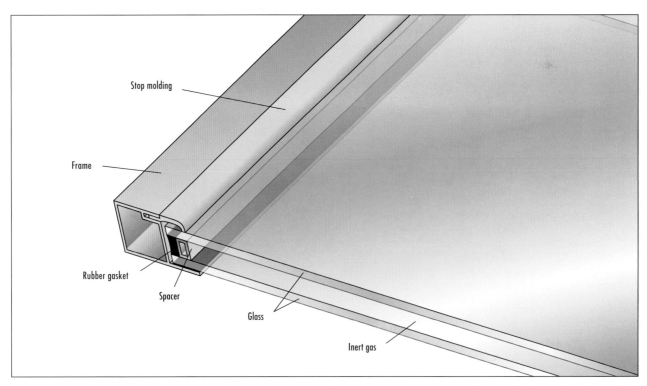

Stop molding

Frame

Rubber gasket

Spacer

Glass

Inert gas

Most newer IGU windows are built with a one-piece frame that has no corner fasteners. The glass unit is pinned into these fixed frames with removable stop molding.

Slide a thin-blade putty knife between one section of stop molding and the sash. Carefully pry the molding out of its channel. Once the first section is removed, the other pieces should be easier to pry free. If the moldings are held in place with brads, pull out the brads with pliers.

Flip the sash over, and slide a razor blade along the seam between the glass and the sash. You may have to do this in several deepening passes to break the bond between the caulk or sealing tape that holds the IGU in place. Work carefully to prevent damaging the sash.

3

4

Use a small paint scraper and mineral spirits to remove the old caulk or setting tape from the sash channel after removing the old IGU.

Apply new strips of sealing tape or a bead of neutral-cure silicone caulk to the sash channel. The tape or caulk should form a continuous seal all around the sash.

5

6

Position the new IGU in the sash channel, pressing it firmly into the tape or caulk to seat it. Make sure the IGU fits into the channel evenly. Use a razor blade to remove excess tape or caulk from the glass.

If the old stop molding strips have been damaged or are in bad repair, cut new ones. Press the stop molding pieces into their channels. Fasten wood stop moldings in place with 1" pneumatic brad nails. Drive the nails at a shallow angle into the sash to avoid hitting the glass.

15. Fixing Sliding Screen Doors

Sliding screen doors easily fall victim to pets and children and often need repair. First you'll need to remove the screen door panel. It is held in grooves by four spring-loaded wheels, one on each corner of the door. Take a short section of the old spline to a hardware store or home center and buy new spline material that matches the diameter of the old one. Also buy replacement screening and an installation tool designed for the size of spline you are installing. These tools come with a roller on both ends: one convex-shaped to force the screen into the door groove, the other concave-shaped to force the spline over the screen.

Screen doors are extremely vulnerable to damage from feet, pets, and a host of other hazards. But fixing them is a breeze with the right tools and a few supplies.

Tools & Materials ▸

Screening material
Mineral spirits
Screwdrivers
Masking tape
Utility knife
Spline roller
Spline cord

Screen Material ▸

Window screening (technically, it's called insect mesh) is woven from three different materials: galvanized wire, aluminum wire, and black fiberglass strands. Each has its advantages and drawbacks: galvanized wire is inexpensive and easy to find, but can become misshapen or rusty; aluminum is less common, but it is strong and won't discolor as easily; fiberglass is easy to work with and won't rust or corrode, but it is prone to tearing. The best advice is simply to buy screening that matches the windows on the rest of your house.

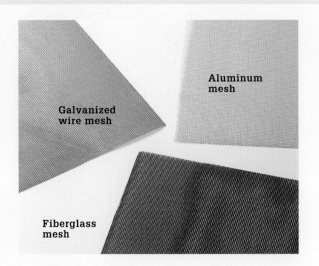

Aluminum mesh

Galvanized wire mesh

Fiberglass mesh

How to Fix a Sliding Screen Door

You can't remove the screen door until you release the tension on the roller wheels. Loosen the adjustment screws, then lift the door out of the channel that holds it captive.

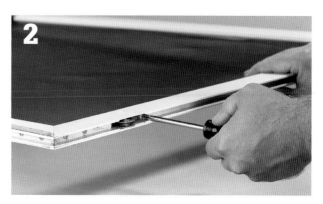

Remove the door rollers using a screwdriver. Sometimes these rollers can just be pried out. Other times you'll have to remove a small screw.

Clean the rollers with mineral spirits and an old paintbrush. Once all the dirt and grime is removed, dry the rollers and lubricate them with light oil.

Pry up one corner of the old spline and then gently pull it out of the screen channel. If this plastic spline is still soft and flexible, it can be reused for the new screen.

Tape the new screen onto the door frame with masking tape. Then make a diagonal cut at each corner to remove the excess screen. This will keep the screen from bulging at the corner when it is pressed into its channel.

Force the screen into the door groove using the convex wheel on the spline roller installation tool. Don't force the screen in with a single pass. Rather, make several lighter passes until the screen reaches the bottom of the channel.

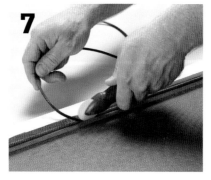

Once the screen is in the channel, install the spline material. Use the concave wheel and work slowly to make sure the spline is forced all the way into the channel. Several passes may be required.

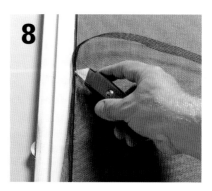

Trim off any excess screening with a sharp utility knife. Do not cut the spline. Reinstall the wheels and replace the panel in the door.

16. Repairing & Maintaining Storm Windows

Compared to removable wood storm windows and screens, repairing combination storm windows is a little more complex. But there are several repairs you can make without too much difficulty, as long as you find the right parts. Take the old corner keys, gaskets, or other original parts to a hardware store that repairs storm windows so the clerk can help you find the correct replacement parts. If you cannot find the right parts, have a new sash built.

Tools & Materials ▶

Tape measure
Screwdriver
Scissors
Drill
Utility knife
Spline roller
Nail set
Hammer
Spline cord
Screening, glass
Rubber gasket
Replacement hardware

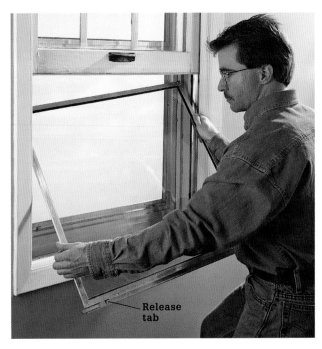

Remove the metal storm window sash by pressing in the release hardware in the lower rail then lifting the sash out. Sash hangers on the corners of the top rail should be aligned with the notches in the side channels before removal.

Release tab

How to Replace Screening in a Metal Storm Window

Pry the vinyl spline from the groove around the edge of the frame with a screwdriver. Retain the old spline if it is still flexible, or replace it with a new spline.

Stretch the new screen tightly over the frame so that it overlaps the edges of the frame. Keeping the screen taut, use the convex side of a spline roller to press the screen into the retaining grooves.

Use the concave side of the spline roller to press the spline into the groove (it helps to have a partner for this). Cut away excess screen using a utility knife.

How to Replace Glass in a Metal Storm Window

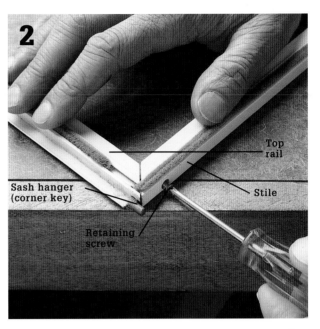

Remove the sash frame from the window, then completely remove the broken glass from the sash. Remove the rubber gasket that framed the old glass pane and remove any glass remnants. Find the dimensions for the replacement glass by measuring between the inside edges of the frame opening, then adding twice the thickness of the rubber gasket to each measurement.

Set the frame on a flat surface, and disconnect the top rail. Remove the retaining screws in the sides of the frame stiles where they join the top rail. After unscrewing the retaining screws, pull the top rail loose, pulling gently in a downward motion to avoid damaging the L-shaped corner keys that join the rail and the stiles. For glass replacement, you need only disconnect the top rail.

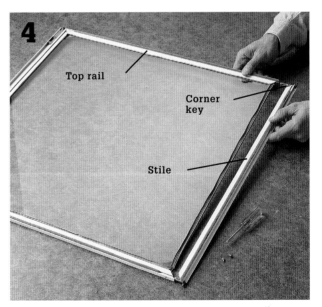

Fit the rubber gasket (buy a replacement if the original is in poor condition) around one edge of the replacement glass pane. At the corners, cut the spine of the gasket partway so it will bend around the corner. Continue fitting the gasket around the pane, cutting at the corners, until all four edges are covered. Trim off any excess gasket material.

Slide the glass pane into the channels in the stiles and bottom rail of the sash frame. Insert corner keys into the top rail, then slip the other ends of the keys into the frame stiles. Press down on the top rail until the mitered corners are flush with the stiles. Drive the retaining screws back through the stiles and into the top rail to join the frame together. Reinsert the frame into the window.

How to Disassemble & Repair a Metal Sash Frame

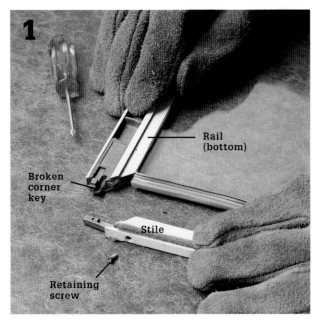

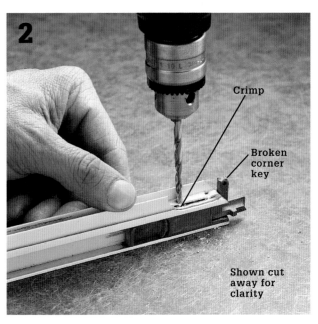

Metal window sash are held together at the corner joints by L-shaped pieces of hardware that fit into grooves in the sash frame pieces. To disassemble a broken joint, start by disconnecting the stile and rail at the broken joint—there is usually a retaining screw driven through the stile that must be removed.

Corner keys are secured in the rail slots with crimps that are punched into the metal over the key. To remove keys, drill through the metal in the crimped area using a drill bit the same diameter as the crimp. Carefully knock the broken key pieces from the frame slots with a screwdriver and hammer.

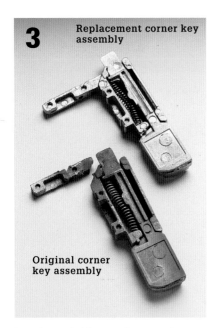

Locate matching replacement parts for the broken corner key, which is usually an assembly of two or three pieces. There are dozens of different types, so it is important that you save the old parts for reference.

Insert the replacement corner key assembly into the slot in the rail. Use a nail set as a punch, and rap it into the metal over the corner key, creating a new crimp to hold the key in place.

Insert the glass and gasket into the frame slots, then reassemble the frame and drive in retainer screws (for screen windows, replace the screening).

Replace turnbuttons and window clips that do not hold storm windows tightly in place. Fill old screw holes with wood dowels and glue before driving the screws.

Lubricate the sliding assemblies on metal-framed combination storm windows or doors once a year using penetrating lubricant.

Replace deteriorated glazing around glass panes in wood-framed windows. Sound glazing makes windows more energy-efficient and more attractive.

Tighten storm door latches by redriving loose screws in the strike plate. If the latch does not catch on the strike plate, loosen the screws on the strike plate, insert thin wood shims between the plate and the jamb, and retighten the screws.

Add a wind chain if your storm door does not have one. Wind chains prevent doors from blowing open too far, causing damage to the door hinges or closer. Set the chain so the door will not open more than 90°.

Adjust the door closer so it has the right amount of tension to close the door securely, without slamming. Most closers have tension-adjustment screws at the end of the cylinder farthest from the hinge side of the door.

17. Weatherizing

No matter whether you live in a hot or a cold climate, weatherizing your home's windows and doors can pay off handsomely. Heating and cooling costs may account for over half of the total household energy bill.

Since most weatherizing projects are relatively inexpensive, you can recover your investment quickly. In fact, in some climates, you can pay back the cost of a weatherproofing project in one season.

If you live in a cold climate, you probably already understand the importance of weatherizing. The value of keeping warm air inside the house during a cold winter is obvious. From the standpoint of energy efficiency, it's equally important to prevent warm air from entering the house during summer.

Weatherizing your home is an ideal do-it-yourself project, because it can be done a little at a time, according to your schedule. In cold climates, the best time of the year to weatherize is the fall, before it turns too cold to work outdoors.

Whether you're concerned about the environment or want to spend less on your utility bills, some simple adjustments around your home can help you accomplish your goal.

Many weatherizing projects deal with windows (pages 93 to 95) because these are the primary areas of heat loss in most homes. Here are a few simple suggestions you might consider for the exterior of your home:

Before buying a basement window well cover, measure the widest point of the window well and note its shape.

Use a caulk that matches your home exterior to seal the window frames.

A felt door sweep can seal out drafts, even if you have an uneven floor or a low threshold.

Minimize heat loss from basement window wells by covering them with plastic window well covers (left, top). Most window well covers have an upper flange designed to slip under the siding. Slip this in place, then fasten the cover to the foundation with masonry anchors and weigh down the bottom flange with stones. For extra weatherizing, seal the edges with caulk.

Adding caulk is a simple way to fill narrow gaps in interior or exterior surfaces. It's also available in a peelable form that can be easily removed at the end of the season.

When buying caulk, estimate half a cartridge per window or door, four for an average-sized foundation sill, and at least one more to close gaps around vents, pipes, and other openings.

Caulk around the outside of the window frames to seal any gaps. For best results, use a caulk that matches or blends with the color of your siding.

There are many different types of caulk and weather stripping materials. All are inexpensive and easy to use, but it's important to get the right materials for the job, as most are designed for specific applications.

Generally, metal and metal-reinforced weather stripping is more durable than products made of plastic, rubber, or foam. However, even plastic, rubber, and foam weather stripping products have a wide range of quality. The best rubber products are those made from neoprene rubber—use this whenever it's available.

A door sweep (previous page, bottom) attaches to the inside bottom of the door to seal out drafts. A felt or bristle sweep is best if you have an uneven floor or a low threshold. Vinyl and rubber models are also available.

A threshold insert fits around the base of the door. Most have a sweep on the interior side and a drip edge on the exterior side to direct water away from the threshold.

A threshold insert seals the gap between the door and the threshold. These are made from vinyl or rubber and can be easily replaced.

Self-adhesive foam strips (below) attach to sashes and frames to seal the air gaps at windows and doors. Reinforced felt strips have a metal spine that adds rigidity in high-impact areas, such as doorstops.

Weatherizing products commonly found in home centers include: A clear film, heat-shrink window insulator kit (A); an aluminum door threshold with vinyl weatherstripping insert (B); a nail-on, rubber door sweep (C); minimal expanding spray foam (D); silicone window and door caulk (E); open-cell foam caulk-backer rod (F); self-adhesive, closed-cell foam weatherstripping coil (G); flexible brass weatherstripping coil, also called V-channel, (H).

18. Detecting Energy Loss

Some of the indications that your home is not energy-efficient will be obvious, such as draftiness, fogged or frosted windows, ice dams, gaps around windows in the foundation wall, and high energy bills. However, it can be more difficult to detect problems such as inadequate wall insulation or the loss of warm air around attic vents. The following are some ways to identify where your home may be losing energy:

- Measure the temperature in different parts of a room. A difference of more than one or two degrees indicates that the room is poorly sealed. The solution is to update the weather stripping around the windows and doors (page 91).
- Check for drafts around windows and doors by holding a tissue next to the jambs on a windy day. If the tissue flutters, the weather stripping is inadequate. Another sign is outside light coming in around the jambs.
- Conduct an energy audit. Most power companies will provide you with an audit kit or conduct an audit for you.
- Monitor your energy usage from year to year. If there's a significant increase that can't be explained by variations in the weather, consider hiring a professional to conduct an energy audit.

The average home has many small leaks, which collectively may add up to the equivalent of a 2-ft. hole in the wall. The air that leaks through these cracks can account for as much as one-third of your total energy loss.

Condensation or frost buildup on windows is a sign of poor weather stripping and an inadequate storm window.

Weather stripping and insulation may begin to deteriorate. Telltale signs include crumbling foam or rubber.

Energy audits done by power companies may use a blower door to measure airflow and detect leaks.

Tips for Weatherizing a Window ▶

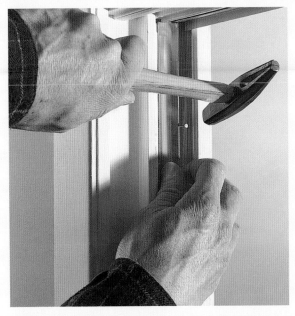

Sliding windows: Treat side-by-side sliding windows as if they were double-hung windows turned 90°. For greater durability, use metal tension strips, rather than self-adhesive compressible foam, in the sash track that fit against the edge of the sash when the window is closed.

Casement windows: Attach self-adhesive foam or rubber compression strips on the outside edges of the window stops.

Storm windows: Create a tight seal by attaching foam compression strips to the outside of storm window stops. After installing the storm window, fill any gaps between the exterior window trim and the storm window with caulk backer rope (left). Check the inside surface of the storm window during cold weather for condensation or frost buildup (facing page). If moisture is trapped between the storm window and the permanent window, drill one or two small holes through the bottom rail (right) to allow moist air to escape. Drill at a slightly upward angle.

How to Weatherstrip a Window

Cut metal V-channel to fit in the channels for the sliding sash, extending at least 2" past the closed position for each sash (do not cover sash-closing mechanisms). Attach the V-channel by driving wire brads (usually provided by the manufacturer) with a tack hammer. Drive the fasteners flush with the surface so the sliding sash will not catch on them.

Flare out the open ends of the V-channels with a putty knife so the channel is slightly wider than the gap between the sash and the track it fits into. Avoid flaring out too much at one time—it is difficult to press V-channel back together without causing some buckling.

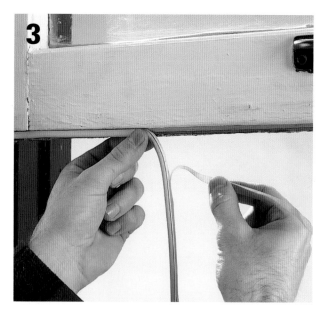

Wipe down the underside of the bottom window sash with a damp rag, and let it dry; then attach self-adhesive compressible foam or rubber to the underside of the sash. Use high-quality hollow neoprene strips, if available. This will create an airtight seal when the window is locked in position.

Bottom sash (raised)

Top sash (lowered)

Seal the gap between the top sash and the bottom sash on double-hung windows. Lift the bottom sash and lower the top sash to improve access, and tack metal V-channel to the bottom rail of the top sash using wire brads. Tip: The open end of the "V" should be pointed downward so moisture cannot collect in the channel. Flare out the V-channel with a putty knife to fit the gap between the sash.

19. Replacing Storm Windows

As old removable storm windows wear out, many homeowners elect to replace them with modern, combination storm windows. Designed to mount permanently in the existing opening, retrofit combination storm windows are very easy to install and are fairly inexpensive.

Most retrofit storm windows attach to the outside edges of the window stops on the sides and top of the window opening. Most windows do not have a bottom stop. Secure the bottom rail of the new window with caulk. Common window sizes are stocked at most building centers, but you may need to order custom-made windows. Have the exact measurements when you order the windows. You also will be asked to choose a finish color and a style. If you have operating double-hung windows, choose three-sash windows so you have the option of opening the top storm sash.

Retrofit storm windows attach to the window stops in the existing window opening. The easiest way to size them is to use the dimensions of old storm windows. Otherwise, measure the narrowest point between the side jambs to find the width, and measure the shortest point from the header to the sill (where it meets the front edges of the stops) to find the height.

Tools & Materials ▸

Screwdriver
Drill
Tape measure
Screws

Replacement storm windows
Caulk or panel adhesive

How to Install a New Combination Storm Window

Buy replacement storm windows to fit your window openings. Test-fit before installing them. To install, first apply a bead of exterior-grade panel adhesive or caulk to the outside edges of the window stops at the top and sides.

Drill pilot holes for the fasteners in the mounting flanges, spaced 12" apart, making sure they will be centered over the stops. Press the new storm window into the opening, centered between the side stops, with the bottom rail resting on the windowsill.

Drive the fasteners (#4 × 1" sheet-metal screws work well), starting at the top. Make sure the window is squarely in the opening, then fill in the fasteners on the side stops. Apply caulk along the bottom rail, leaving a ¼"-wide gap midway as a weep hole.

Creative Publishing international

Copyright © 2010
Creative Publishing international, Inc.
400 First Avenue North, Suite 300
Minneapolis, Minnesota 55401
1-800-328-0590
www.creativepub.com
All rights reserved

Printed in China

10 9 8 7 6 5 4 3 2 1

President/CEO: Ken Fund

Home Improvement Group

Publisher: Bryan Trandem
Managing Editor: Tracy Stanley
Senior Editor: Mark Johanson

Creative Director: Michele Lanci-Altomare
Art Direction/Design: Jon Simpson, Brad Springer, James Kegley

Lead Photographer: Joel Schnell
Set Builder: James Parmeter
Production Managers: Laura Hokkanen, Linda Halls

Page Layout Artist: Lisa Beavers

Here's How: Windows
Created by: The Editors of Creative Publishing international, Inc., in cooperation with Black & Decker. Black & Decker® is a trademark of The Black & Decker Corporation and is used under license.